THE SECOND FIRST ART:

POETRY IN TRANSLATION AND ESSAYS ON THE ART OF TRANSLATING IN HONOR OF AARON KRAMER

Susan L. Rosenstreich, Editor
Ann Steinmetz, Special Editor for Poetry
Elio Zappulla, Special Editor for Essays

EDITIONS D'AUTRUI
Southold, New York

Copyright 1996 by EDITIONS D'AUTRUI
Southold, New York

All rights reserved under International Copyright Conventions.

Copyright to all translations in this volume is held by the translators and permission to print or reprint them is hereby gratefully acknowledged. Special permission to publish some of the translations was granted by the following:

Manolis Anagnostakis for **EPILOG**
Arnoldo Mondadori Editore for **ULYSSES** by Umberto Saba

ISBN 0-934477-01-9

TABLE OF CONTENTS

Introduction..1
   Susan L. Rosenstreich

PART I: Poetry in Translation in Honor of Aaron Kramer

Introduction: FRAGILE POEM, IRON SONG..................................4
   Susan L. Rosenstreich and Ann Steinmetz

TO A SAXON POET..7
   Jorge Luis Borges
   Translated by Dick Barnes

AN AFGHAN WOMAN TESTIFIES...8
   Anonymous
   Translated by Daniela Gioseffi

THE MESSAGE..11
   Anonymous
   Translated by Aaron Kramer

MORNING SONG...13
   Hamutal Bar Yosef
   Translated by Shirley Kaufman

LAMENT TO THE SPIRIT OF WAR..14
   Enheduanna
   Translated by Daniela Gioseffi

From COUNTERSONG TO WALT WHITMAN.............................15
   Pedro Mir
   Translated by Jonathan Cohen

UNTITLED..26
   Simonides
   Translated by Charles Plumb

AMID BIRDS OF PREY...27
    Friedrich Nietzche
    Translated by Siegfried Mandel

THE POET FIRDUSI..32
    Heinrich Heine
    Translated by Aaron Kramer

ICARUS..39
    Philippe Desportes
    Translated by Charles Plumb

SLAUGHTERED VILLAGE..40
    Salem Jubran
    Translated by Walter M. Barzelay

PALESTINIAN BOY..41
    Walter M. Barzelay
    Translated by the Poet

CHILDREN...43
    Yosef Sharon
    Translated by Linda Zisquit

FROM A CHILDHOOD..45
    Rainer Maria Rilke
    Translated by Vern Rutsala

JOSEPH'S SUSPICION...46
    Rainer Maria Rilke
    Translated by Norbert Krapf

(#286) ABOUT STALIN..47
    Osip Mandel'shtam
    Translated by Paul T. Hopper

THE MADMAN..48
    S. J. Pretorius
    Translated by John Brander

DIARY (THE LAST THOUGHTS OF KAFKA'S SISTER)............50
    Adrian Paunescu
    Translated by Eva Feiler & Stanley Barkan

ULYSSES..51
    Umberto Saba
    Translated by Elio Zappulla

From UNDER THE INFLUENCE OF THE MANDOLIN............52
    Zalman Schne'or
    Translated by Abraham Almany

CRITIC..56
    Johann Wolfgang von Goethe
    Translated by James Schevill

EPITAPH...57
    Eugene Scribe
    Translated by James Schevill

UNTITLED..58
    Pir Sultan Abdal
    Translated by P.N. Remler

A Variation on Catullus's ODI ET AMO......................................60
    Gaius Valerius Catullus
    Translated by James Schevill

OAKS AND ROSES..61
    Sarah Kirsch
    Translated by Charles Fishman and Marina Roscher

WINTER'S END..63
    Dan Pagis
    Translated by Robert Friend and Shimon Sandbank

REQUIEM FOR THE MISSING...64
    Victor Rivera Toledo
    Translated by Luis Eduardo Rivera

I AM BLACK..66
     Rado
     Translated by Jerome Brooks and Raymond Patterson

ON MY STREET..67
     Portugese Fado
     Translated by Rhonda Cunha and Carlos Cunha

SAVEZ-VOUS PLANTER LES CHOUX?..69
     French Children's Song
     Translated by Ruth Rubin

SNOW..71
     H. Leivich
     Translated by Harold Black

THIS IS YOU..72
     Johannes Edfelt
     Translated by David Ignatow and Leif Sjoberg

PORTENTS..73
     Folke Isaacson
     Translated by Stephen Klass and Leif Sjoberg

I'D LOVE TO LOVE LOVING..75
     Fernando Pessoa
     Translated by Edwin Honig

BALLAD OF HRDLICKA'S WITCH..76
     Frederick Brainin
     Translated by the Poet

SONG IN A DEAD LANGUAGE..78
     Nikolai Kantchev
     Translated by Bradley R. Strahan and Pamela Perry

THE SECONDS..80
     Hirsh Osherovitch
     Translated by Seymour Levitan

UPROOTED..81
    Jacob Sternberg
    Translated by Seymour Levitan

SEARCHING FOR HOME..82
    Friedrich Schnack
    Translated by Norbert Krapf

THE PRODIGAL SON..83
    Roman Bar-Or
    Translated by Barry Wallenstein

AFTERWARDS..84
    Harry Martinson
    Translated by W.H. Auden and Leif Sjoberg

EIN LEBEN..85
    Don Pagis
    Translated by Robert Friend and Shimon Sandbank

I ACCEPT..86
    Rado
    Translated by Jerome Brooks and Raymond Patterson

FROM THE AFTERWORLD..87
    Sachiko Yoshihara
    Translated by William Stafford and Yorifumi Yaguchi

QUIETNESS LIGHT DARKNESS..89
    Li Po
    Translated by John Tagliabue

THE NIGHTINGALE..90
    Marie de France
    Translated by Miriam Baker

RAZGLEDNICA..97
    Miklos Radnoti
    Translated by Timea Szell

EPILOG..98
    Manolis Anagnostakis
    Translated by Sam Abrams

PART II: Essays on the Art of Translating in Honor of Aaron Kramer

Introduction: TRADUTTORE, TRADITORE............................101
    Elio Zappulla

PHOENICIA, MALTESE AND POETRY...................................103
    Charles Mizzi

TRANSLATING THE ESKIMOS..107
    Edward Field

**LANGUAGE AS HOMELAND, OR FINDING
THE AMERICAN VOICE**..112
    Claire Nicolas White

TRANSLATING WITH W.H. AUDEN..116
    Leif Sjoberg

ON TRANSLATING SONGS...131
    Ruth Rubin

SOME PROBLEMS IN TRANSLATION....................................135
    Paul Forchheimer

**THE TRANSLATOR AND THE MULTILINGUAL
TEXT: TWO VERSIONS OF UMBERTO
ECO'S "NOME DELLA ROSA"**......................................139
    Fritz Hensey

TRANSLATION: THE PROBLEM OF PURPOSE.................151
    Richard E. Braun

ON TRANSLATING..170
    Martin Tucker

THE MAKING OF ARTISTS: A TRANSLATOR'S WORK...........174
   Donald Gilzinger

NOTES ON CONTRIBUTORS..194

INTRODUCTION:
FIRST ART, SECOND ART, AND AARON KRAMER

Susan L. Rosenstreich

The distinguished career of Aaron Kramer entered a new period of synthesis in 1989, when he reduced the number of hours he devoted to classroom teaching. After more than thirty years as a professor of English at Adelphi University, at Queens College and, finally, at Dowling College, Aaron had brought to his students the excitement and inspiration of poetry in its finest embodiment as first among the arts. In addition to meeting the demands of his teaching responsibilities, he had maintained a steady pace of writing and translating poetry, as well as a continued program of scholarly publication. His decision to devote less time to the classroom provided an appropriate occasion to pause and summarize what it was that his teaching and writing had communicated, and this volume of poetry in translation and essays on the art of translating is a partial harvest of that moment.

Donald Gilzinger, whose bibliographic essay on Aaron's works appears in the second half of this book, has said that the range of genres and wealth of material of his subject present a unique challenge to a bibliographer. But if it is a challenge to annotate and categorize the elements of this body of work, it is less difficult to appreciate its concerns. In collections of poetry, in anthologies of translations to which he is a principal or sole contributor, in critical studies, and in countless lectures and public readings, Aaron has given careful articulation to his preoccupations. They appear clearly when, assessing the commitment of nineteenth century American poets to the prophetic tradition, he writes that the best of these escaped the "contagious meanness" of their contemporaries.[1]

The high principle these poets invoked in their work becomes simultaneously the object of their art and the subject of it, as long as they translated noble thought into poetry. Reading Whitman and Thoreau in this manner, Aaron gave powerful expression to convictions about the subject matter of good poetry, and made clear to his audience what the first art really is. No longer is the poem, or any created object, for that matter, the boundary of its artistic character; the art object is, rather, subsequent to an earlier and first creation unique to the artist. This first creation is the vision of a world devoid of "contagious meanness", and emerges as a thought before it suggests itself as an object.

In this view of poetry, and of art, in general, taking that highly aimed vision out of its imagined state into its created state constitutes the artist's work. This process is, strictly speaking, translation, then poetry, or painting, or sculpture. So it seems that, in the abstract sense, Aaron has always considered translation as the second first art. Even after the art object has been realized, the abstract notion of translation continues to operate, developing awareness and appreciation of the thing created.

But Aaron's study of American poets also raises the issue of translation in its common sense of bringing words from their source language into a target language. One of the links between the two definitions of translation is the matter of first and second arts. The first definition of translation in its abstract sense addresses translation as the creation of a work of art. In the second, more commonly accepted sense, translation involves the transfer of a written work from one language to another. Though he was not referring to this second sense of translating, Gerard Manley Hopkins fashioned an elegant paradigm through which we might appreciate shared characteristics of the two.

Hopkins organized a poem into "overthought", its so-called explicit meaning, and "underthought", its supposed implicit meaning. Such organization provides translators of poetry with a protocol for the ordering of their tasks, allowing them to attend to "overthought" as a problem of explicit word meaning, and to "underthought" as it pertains to a poem's web of word meanings that communicate its implicit meaning. In an obvious sense, this extends the common meaning of translation into the domain of the second first art. It is second because it is preceded by the poem in another language.

Yet another resemblance between the process of avoiding "contagious meanness", and the paradigm of explicit and implicit meanings is their mutual focus on thought in poetry. It further explicates Aaron's fundamental concern for intellect in poetry, but above all, it deepens our understanding of the relationship between poetry and translation in his career.

Both these pursuits place thought in the center of the process that culminates in a poem. In writing good poetry, noble thought is translated into language. In translating good poetry, noble thought is translated into another language. And to accomplish either, an individual needs to distinguish "overthought" from "underthought". In both cases, concerns about language are addressed by referring to the initial thought, be it that of the poet, or that which the translator imagined the poet to have had. Considered from the perspective of second first arts, Aaron's career has, thus far, produced a synthesis of poetry and translation that attacks "contagious meanness".

Where might the next phase of this career lead? Besides reflecting the history of Aaron's contributions to translation and poetry, the pages that follow also suggest directions in which he appears to be evolving. The overwhelming majority of poems selected to appear in this book deals with the anger of powerless people. And several essays point to the high calling of translation in counteracting abuses of power. Because the "contagious meanness" of our own time bears on these issues, some of Aaron's most recent work has examined them in the light of contemporary events.

Shifting forces in geographical regions with histories of unrest and repression account for a great portion of the material in this book. These regions have been of long-term interest to Aaron, and current events have prompted him to participate in fresh interpretations of history. The excitement of the opportunity to review, and at times to revise, his thinking on the role of the poet and the array of choices the poet has at any given moment is apparent in his lectures and poetry readings these days.

And, of course, there is always the matter of art. It is the matter of making the one object that will speak at one time to all, of calling forth in one succinct word the best of human effort, of righting in one corrective the habit of hurting those who least deserve it, of breaking the chain of "contagious meanness". As teacher, poet, and translator, Aaron has set the standard for this matter of art. We have grown as a result of art that meets this standard, and now, as he devotes more of his time to the work of poet and translator, we look forward to the new synthesis that will emerge from his creativity.

---

[1] Aaron Kramer, The Prophetic Tradition in American Poetry, 1835-1900, (Cranbury, New Jersey: Associated University Presses, Inc.,) p. 355.

INTRODUCTION: FRAGILE POEM, IRON SONG: POETRY IN TRANSLATION IN HONOR OF AARON KRAMER

Susan L. Rosenstreich & Ann Steinmetz

The poems in translation gathered here in honor of Aaron Kramer come from his friends, his colleagues, his former students. There are 49 of them, translated from 21 languages, some dead for centuries, such as the Sumerian from which Daniela Gioseffi translated **LAMENT TO THE SPIRIT OF WAR** attributed to the priestess Enheduanna, or dead in the mind of the poet, as is painfully evident in Nikolai Kantchev's **SONG IN A DEAD LANGUAGE**, translated here by Bradley R. Strahan with Pamela Perry, or, as in the case of the very language of poetry in **EPILOG** by Manolis Anagnostakis, possibly dying even as the poem is being read.

Yet, fragile as they may be, these poems pulse with life in the English version brought to us by their translators. Be they the thoughts of a mind as great as that of Friedrich Nietszche, or the passion in a breast as humble as Zalman Schne'or's, they wait for us, their English-language readers, to relay their ardent messages of love or hate or fear or hope. Harivanshrai Bachchan, the much-revered Hindi poet and former minister of foreign affairs for India, made poetry into an extended metaphor for its power to move us. For Bachchan, that power was so great as to cause us to lose ourselves to it, to forget who we are and to awaken as more than we were. As Prem Prasad, one of Bachchan's translators, has rendered his words from **MADHUSHALA** in which this metaphor is developed: "You offer and then withdraw,/ I touch you with my lips and you are not there./ Forward, backward, where am I? Where will I be?" In this brief excerpt from a longer poem, for which the translator was unable to receive translation rights, and which we were therefore unable to reprint in its entirety, we struggle alongside the poet against the world as we imagine it and listen as he gives voice to our desire to possess and control it. The humorous adage that poetry is what is lost in the translation seems curiously out of harmony with these words in translation, for there is such vitality in them that it is difficult to imagine what is missing.

The vitality of these translations is apparent also in the proliferation of forms in which the poetry appears. Georgos Seferis' **PANTOUM**, which Carrie Lecakes and Antonia Raptis have brought into English, is itself a Greek variety of a verse form thought to have originated in Southeast Asia.

In this verse form, the second and fourth lines of each quatrain are repeated as the first and third lines of the following one. Seferis, a Greek diplomat who eventually denounced the military regime of his country, and who received the Nobel Prize for literature in 1963, was preceded by Victor Hugo, Leconte de Lisle and Charles Baudelaire in the use of the pantoum in the nineteenth and twentieth centuries. We did not succeed in obtaining copyright permission on behalf of the translators to reproduce their entire version in this anthology, but to illustrate our point, we reprint here the following excerpt from it:

> The night narrows and stands like a foreigner
> The lights have blacked out over the black silk
> My soul you recognize --- Law ties you
> And what will remain and what
> Will leave you.
>
> Blackness between the lights, turn off.
> You hear only the years
> And what will remain and what
> Will leave you
> If luck lights the dumbfounded loophole.

Nor can it be said that the prose of Johannes Edfelt's **THIS IS YOU** is any less poetic than the rhyming couplets in Heinrich Heine's **THE POET FIRDUSI**. **AN AFGHAN WOMAN TESTIFIES** is a letter and **ON MY STREET** is a song. That such a range should be so broad yet be known as poetry attests to the heady and synergic drive of poet, translator and reader to seek and find in the words on the page something that outlasts and transcends the everyday, familiar world.

If the breadth of substance and the wealth of forms emphasize this poetry's remarkable vigor, the insistent presence of heritage dramatizes the source of inspiration to which poet and translator respond on these pages. To frame the translations that follow, we chose poems that address this very notion of the mutual heritage of poetry and translation. The rich significance of Jorge Luis Borges' opening poem **TO A SAXON POET**, originally in Spanish, and translated here by an American, is meant to establish the context for our reflection on the complexities of cultures meeting across time, as well as across space. We end with Manolis Anagnostakis' plaintive description of what we lose when we live in a world without poetry. But he might as well have said that we lose as much in a world without translation. For by translating this poem, Sam Abrams dispels Anagnostakis' greatest fear. "(T)he last lines ever/ The last poets will write to the last readers" have not yet been written as long as the translator continues the work of those who created the world of poetry. Yes, the poetry these "last lines" inscribe on the page has a fragile life, but it is the life of the "iron song" Borges heard when he spoke to the Saxon poet of long ago, a song kept strong by those who bring it to us in a language as true to the original poems as the translators can make it.

TO A SAXON POET

JORGE LUIS BORGES

Known in the United States mainly for his fiction, Jorge Luis Borges is recognized in the Spanish-speaking world as a great poet. Perhaps his forthcoming **SELECTED POEMS,** *translated by Robert Mezey and Dick Barnes, will clarify our notion of his achievement.*

Snow fallen on Northumberland has known
And lost the footprints that you made in passing
And suns and stars have set past numbering,
My gray brother, between your hour and mine.

Slowly, in slow shade, you forged laborious
Metaphor of swordblade in the seas,
Of living horror hidden in the forest,
And of the solitude that dogs our days.

Where can I find your deeds, your name, your birth?
They are all long sealed in oblivion.
I'll never know you as you must have been

When you were a man like me and walked the earth.
Lone exile was the road you trudged along.
Now you are nothing but your iron song.

TRANSLATED BY DICK BARNES FROM SPANISH

AN AFGHAN WOMAN TESTIFIES

An Anonymous Poet

An anonymous Afghan woman who was shot fleeing with her daughters from a prison camp in Kabul scribbled this testimony. It was found in a refugee camp by a journalist who brought it out of the country to be translated. Malali, Naheed, and Rabia Balkhi, mentioned in the fragment, were poets and activists who died in the Afghan resistance.

Our faces thrust between the bars of the prison gate,
we wait,
clinging to cold iron, a crown of women, worrying
if we will see our husbands, sons, brothers, again.
My son is inside the stone walls with his father
for whom he carried his gun.

At last the names of political prisons are posted.
The women's eyes strain in the cold,
their sockets as frozen as the ground under the prayer rugs
the old men bring to the gate to pray for sons, nephews,
grandchildren who are tortured or executed inside the walls,
among the many men who chose the freedom of their god or death.
I've told no one such blasphemy,
but my husband is my only god,
my son, my only prince of heaven.
Outside the walls, we wait and wail and hope
and a woman screams from behind her veil, seeing
that her son's name, her husband's, too, are there

among the executed.
We know there are no more men left in her family
or she would not be here alone. Only
the women who have no men
come to the prison gate alone.
I am not so lucky as to know my fate.
No heroine like Naheed,
I carry no flag like Malalai.
No poet like Rabia Balkhi, I simply wait in worry and hate.
Today again I go to return again in the morning to wait and wait
and wait...my mind hanging from a thread
like the rag the old woman makes tearing at her veil as she weeps—
exposing her withered face in the madness of grief.
Heavy with our own, we can do nothing for her but let her weep.
Perhaps we envy her tears because, at least, she knows her fate.
While we still wait heavy with the weight of holding our vigil
at the cold iron gate.
To find my way through the street, I must pass the old palace again,
where the guards display blood-soaked rugs.
They drag me into the palace from the street to show me where
women and children were massacred by soldiers yesterday.
They show me to warn me to stay in the camp and behave.
I make it back to the camp, sick with hunger and disgust.
My daughters with mangled fingers
frostbitten from the winter cold wait for me by the camp gate.
My words are useless. I will be dead when you read them.
They are mere facts of my life, not poetry.
I am a woman who dared to dream of love, of poetry,

of reading. I taught myself to write,
hour after hour before the firelight.
When you read these works, I will be dead.
I've decided that when I see my husband's name,
my son's among the executed of the prison,
I will tear my veil from my face,
take my daughters with me into the frozen mountains.
We will run and the bullets will fly after us
and set us free from this wait to be free.

TRANSLATED BY DANIELA GIOSEFFI FROM AFGHAN

THE MESSAGE
FROM "THE BATTLE OF MALDON"

An Anonymous Poet of the Anglo-Saxon Chronicle

THE BATTLE OF MALDON is an anonymous account of a 991 battle in which the men of Essex in present-day England were defeated by a predatory force under Olaf Tryggvason at the mouth of the Blackwater River. It is an entry in the Anglo-Saxon Chronicle, a year-by-year journal of events, begun under Alfred the Great. Scholars believe the unknown poet was well-versed in the epic tradition and had probably witnessed the battle or received firsthand reports of it.

There stood at the river bank, bellowing sternly,

a man of the raiders, ready with words.

Menacingly he mouthed their message

straight at the stalwart across the stream:

"The seamen have sent me, and asked me to say —

the treasures you own, you must turn them over

to win our protection; wiser it is

at once to buy off this battle with tribute

than force us to deal you so fierce a fray.

No killing each other, if you come across quickly;

we'll grant a truce in exchange for gold.

If you, who are greatest here, will agree

to pay the ransom and rescue your people,

to give the sea-goers, as glory due them,

treasures for peace — a proper trade —
we'll take the tribute back to our boats,
set out to sea, and seal your safety."
Byrhtnoth roared back, raised high the shield,
brandished his blade, his slender spear;
furious, firm, was the answer he flung:
"This people's reply — do you hear it, pirate?
Spears are the gift you'll get from us,
veteran swords with points of venom,
gear that will give you no gain in battle.
Seafarer spokesman, return to your troops;
bring them our will, let them burst at the words:
here, unalarmed, stands the lord with his legions,
firm in defense of their fatherland —
the realm of my ruler, Aethelred's realm,
his soil and his sowers; the pagan shall perish
in battle. Too base it would be, I think,
that you should go back to your boats with our booty
unchallenged, raiders, now you have chanced
to come this long way across our country;
nor may we permit you such light-won loot;
sword-point, not riches, shall reconcile us —
trial of arms, before tribute is taken!"

TRANSLATED BY AARON KRAMER FROM OLD ENGLISH

MORNING SONG

Hamutal Bar Yosef

Hamutal Bar Yosef, a native-born Israeli, divides her time between Tel Aviv, Jerusalem and Beersheva, where she teaches Hebrew Literature at the Ben Gurion University of the Negev. She is the author of four prize-winning collections of Hebrew poetry.

Get up get up the vivid green forests are burning

the sour feast of the orchards is burning

geese in the coop honk without knowing

they're burning alive

get up get up

the delicate embroidery at the edge of the silk sheet is burning

and the white cotton you're wearing it too is burning fast

your face is already scorched with carbonized dust

your mind flies in the air like a plague

while you breathe and you hear

get up get up get out

Translated by Shirley Kaufman from Hebrew

LAMENT TO THE SPIRIT OF WAR

Enheduanna

Enheduanna (ca. 2300 B.C.) was a Sumerian priestess or shaman who worshipped the goddess Inanna, dedicating her works to her. She is the first known poet, man or woman, of prehistoric times whose works have been preserved in artifact.

You hack everything down in battle...
You slice away the land and charge
    disguised as a raging storm,
growl as a roaring hurricane,
yell like a tempest yells,
thunder, rage, roar, and drum,
expel evil winds!
Your feet are filled with anxiety!

Like a fiery monster you fill the land with poison.
As a rage from the sky,
you growl over the earth,
and trees and bushes collapse before you.
You are as blood rushing down a mountain,
spirit of hate, greed and anger,
dominator of heaven and earth!
Your fire wafts over our tribe,
mounted on a beast,
with indomitable commands,
you decide all fate.
You triumph over all our rites.
Who can fathom you?

Translated by Daniela Giosefei from Sumerian

From
COUNTERSONG TO WALT WHITMAN
(SONG OF OURSELVES)

PEDRO MIR

Poet Laureate of the Dominican Republic, Pedro Mir is considered to be one of the most important Latin American poets of our time. His first book in English translation, COUNTERSONG TO WALT WHITMAN AND OTHER POEMS, was published by Azul Editions.

<u>1</u>.
There once was a virgin wilderness.
Trees and land without names or fences.
There once was a perfect wilderness.
Many years ago. Long before the ancestors of our ancestors.
The plains played with galloping buffalo.
The endless coasts played with pearls.
The rocks let loose diamonds from their wombs.
And the hills played with goats and gazelles . . .

The breeze would swirl through clearings in the woods
heavy with the bold play of deer and birch trees
filling the pores of evening with seed.
And it was a virgin land filled with surprises.
Wherever a clod of earth touched a seed
all of a sudden there grew a sweet-smelling forest.

At times it was assaulted by a frenzy of pollen
squeezing out the poplars, the pines, the fir trees,
and pouring night and landscapes into clusters.
And there were caverns and woods and prairies
teeming with brooks and clouds and animals.

<u>2.</u>
(O luminous-bearded Walt Whitman . . . !)
It was the spacious Far West and the Mississippi and the Rockies
and the Great Valley of East Tennessee
and the woods of Maine and the hills of Vermont
and the flats along the coasts and more . . .

                                                And missing
were only man's fevers and his head.
   All that was missing was for the word

                                                      mine
to go deep inside the caverns and caves
and fall into the furrow and kiss the North
Star. And for every man
               to carry on his chest
under his arm, in his eyes and on his shoulders,
his abundant I,
                                his permanence
in himself.
and to spill it out on that wild and savage land.

<u>6</u>.
O Walt Whitman, your sensitive beard
was a net in the wind!
It throbbed and filled with ardent figures
of sweethearts and youths, of brave souls and farmers,
of country boys walking to creeks,
of rowdies wearing spurs and maidens wearing smiles,
of the hurried marches of numberless beings,
of tresses or hats . . .

And you went on listening
road after road,
striking their heartstrings
word after word.
O Walt Whitman of guileless beard,
I've come through the years to your red blaze of fire!

7.
Men went onward, with their fate
that was robust and manly,
                  sweaty. They piloted boats
and days. On the way they fought with Indian braves
and squaws. At night they told their tales and spoke
of towns. Out in the breeze they hung their shirts
and roads. In the valleys they put their stagecoaches
and towns. Out in the breeze they hung their shirts
and the odor of their chests from swinging the axe
and sometimes they got lost in the shade
of a woman's waist . . .
That land was growing upwards
and downwards.
              Skyscrapers
                                    and mines
kept leaving the earth's surface,
                          united and distant.
The strongest ones, the brightest ones, the ones
most capable of blazing a trail, went onward.
Others stayed behind. But the march
went on with no rest, no looking back.

Self-confidence
> was essential.

Faith
> was essential.

And ever so gently was forged the song:
I the cowboy and I the adventurer
and I the pioneer and I the gold panner
and I Alvin, I William with my name and my luck at cards,
and I the preacher with my baritone voice
and I the maiden who have my face
and I the prostitute who have my figure
and I the merchant, captain of my silver
and I
> the human being

in pursuit of fortune for myself, above me,
behind me.
> And with the whole world

at my feet, subject to my voice,
gathered on my back
 and the heights of the mountain range I
 and the wheat of the prairie I
 and the glint of the plows I
 and the banks of the streams I
 and the heart of the amethyst I
and I,
 Walt Whitman,
> a kosmos,

of Manhattan the son . . . !

2.
For
What has a great undeniable poet been,
>	but a crystal-clear pool
>	>	where a people discover their perfect likeness?
What has he been
>	but a deep garden
>	>	where all men recognize themselves through language?
And what
>	but the chord of a boundless guitar
>	>	where the fingers of the people play
>	>	>	their simple, their own, their strong and
>	>	>	>	true, innumerable song?
For that's why you, numerous Walt Whitman, who saw and ranted
just the right word for singing your people,
who in the middle of the night said

>	>	>	>	I

and the fisherman understood himself in his slicker
and the hunter heard himself in the midst of his shot
and the woodcutter recognized himself in his axe
and the farmer in his freshly sown field and the gold
panner in his yellow reflection on the water
and the maiden in her future town
>	>	>	growing and maturing
under her skirt
and the prostitute in her fountain of gaiety
and the miner of darkness in his steps beneath his homeland . . .
When the tall preacher, bowing his head,
between two long hands, said

>   I

and found himself united with the foundryman and the salesman,
with the obscure traveler in a soft cloud of dust,
with the dreamer and the climber,
with the earthy mason resembling a stone slab,
with the farmer and the weaver,
with the sailor in white resembling a handkerchief . . .
And all the people saw themselves
when they heard the word
>   I

and all the people recognized themselves in your song
when they heard the word
>   I, Walt Whitman, a kosmos
>   of Manhattan the son . . . !

Because you were the people, you were I,
and I was Democracy, the people's family name,
and I was also Walt Whitman, a kosmos,

of Manhattan the son . . . !

<u>11</u>.
Ask the night and the wine and the dawn about it . . .
Out around the hills of Vermont, the flats along the coasts,
throughout the spacious Far West and the Rockies,
throughout the Great Valley of East Tennessee and the woods of Maine,
Go through the furniture and automobile plants, the docks,
the mines, the apartment houses, the celestial elevators,
the brothels, the instruments of artists;
look for an obscure piano, pull apart the chords,
the hammers, the keyboard, break its silent harp
and cast it upon the last rails of the dawn . . .

No use.
You'll never find the pure sound of the word

                                      I.

Smash a telephone and a phonograph record,
tear out the wires from a loudspeaker at night,
take the soul of a Stradivarius out into the sun . . .
No use.
You'll never find the pure sound of the word

                                      I.

(O Walt Whitman, of tattered beard!)
What about the fallen faces, what about the silenced tongues,
what about the defeated guts and the ruined arteries . . . !
You'll never find

                 again

                           the flawless sound

of the word

                                      I.

<u>13</u>.
If you want to find the harsh modern sound
of the word

                I

                           go to Santo Domingo.
Pass through Nicaragua. Ask around in Honduras.

Listen to Peru, to Bolivia, to Argentina.
Everywhere you will run into a high-sounding captain

                                  an I.

A shining leader,

                an I, a kosmos.
A God-sent man,
                an I, a kosmos, a son of his homeland.
And in the middle of the deafening night of America
you will hear, behind ripe things and sweet smells,
mixed with faint moans, with swearwords and shouts,
with sobs and fists, with long tears and long
bristles and long curses
                an I, Walt Whitman, a kosmos,
                of Manhattan the son.
An old song turned into the song of force
among the gears of the factories, in the streets
of the cities. An I, a kosmos, in the cane fields,
and in the railroad cars and in the sugar mills.
An old song turned into the song of blood and misery,
an I, a Walt Whitman, a kosmos,
of Manhattan the son . . . !

<u>15</u>.
And now
it is no longer the word

                                          I

The accomplished word
the password to begin the world.
And now
now it is the word

                        we.
And now,
now has come the hour of the countersong.
        We the railroad workers,
        we the students,

we the miners,
we the peasants,
we the poor of the earth,
the populators of the world,
the heroes of everyday work,
with our love and our fists,
enamored of hope.
We the white-skinned,
the black-skinned, the yellow-skinned,
the Indians, the copper-skinned,
the Moorish and dark-skinned,
the red-skinned and the olive-skinned,
the blonds and platinum blonds,
united by work,
by misery, by silence,
by the cry of a solitary man
who in the middle of the night,
with a perfect whip,
with a humble income,
with a golden knife and an iron face,
wildly cries out

                                          I

and hears the crystal-clear echo
of a shower of blood
that decidedly feeds on us

                                        we the people

in the middle of the piers moving away

                                        we the people

and below the horizon of the factories

                                        we the people

in the flower, in the pictures, in the tunnels

                                        we the people

in the tall structure on the way to orbits

                                                  we the people

on the way to marble halls

                                                  we the people

on the way to prisons

                                                    we . . .

<u>17</u>.

Why did you want to listen to a poet?

I am speaking to all of you.

To those who came to isolate him from his people,
to separate him from his blood and his land,
to flood his road.
Those who drafted him into the army.
The ones who defiled his luminous beard and put a gun
on his shoulders that were loaded with maidens and pioneers.
The ones who do not want Walt Whitman the democrat
but another Whitman, atomic and savage.
The ones who want to outfit him with boots
to crush the heads of nations.
To grind into blood the temples of little girls.
To smash into atoms the old man's flesh.
The ones who take the tongue of Walt Whitman
for a sign of spraying bullets,
for a flag of fire.
No, Walt Whitman, here are the poets of today
aroused to justify you!
" - - Poets to come! . . . Arouse!   For you must justify me."
Here we are, Walt Whitman, to justify you.
Here we are
                      for you
                                        asking for peace.

The peace you needed
to drive the world with your song.
Here we are
                      saving your hills of Vermont,
your woods of Maine, the sap and fragrance of your land,
your spurred rowdies, your smiling maidens,
your country boys walking to creeks.
Saving them, Walt Whitman, from the tycoons
who take your language for the language of war.
No, Walt Whitman, here are the poets of today,
workers of today, pioneers of today, peasants
of today,
              firm and roused to justify you!
O Walt Whitman of aroused beard!
Here we are without beards,

without arms, without ears,
without any strength in our lips,
spied on,
red and persecuted,
full of eyes
wide open throughout the islands,
full of courage, of knots of pride
untied through all the nations,
with your sign and your language, Walt Whitman
here we are,
standing up
to justify you,
of Manhattan our constant companion!

                TRANSLATED BY JONATHAN COHEN FROM SPANISH

From SIMONIDES

SIMONIDES

Born about 556 B.C. on the Greek island now known as Kea, Simonides gained fame as a Greek lyric poet during the time of Pindar and Aeschylus.

Casting upon their country fame - stronger than fire

themselves these men assumed the dark mantle of death

Nor are they dead, these dead - their valour soaring aloft

leads them from that mansion in a gleaming light.

TRANSLATED BY CHARLES PLUMB FROM ANCIENT GREEK

AMID BIRDS OF PREY

Friedrich Nietzsche

Friedrich Nietzsche (1844-1900), best known as a philosopher with enormous impact on modern writers from D.H. Lawrence to Thomas Mann, also wrote poetry. "Amid Birds of Prey" is a poem in **DIONYSUS DITHYRAMBS**, *and reflects the poet's last, lonely steps to madness.*

Whoever wishes to descend here,
how rapidly
the depths will swallow him.
— But you, Zarathustra, even now
isn't it that, like the fir tree
you love the abyss? —

It plunges its roots where
the cliff itself shudders;
looking into the depths —,
it hesitates at the brinks
where everything roundabout
wants to descend:
between impatience,
wild rocks, cascading streams
patient, accepting, hard, silent,
lonely ...

<u>Solitary</u>!
who would even dare

to be a guest here,
<u>your</u> guest?...
a bird of prey, maybe,
that surely would imbed itself
with glee
in the hair of the sturdy endurer,
with mad laughter —
the bird-of-prey's laughter ...

"<u>Why</u> be so steadfast?"
— he mocks cruelly:
one must have wings,
if one
        loves the abyss...
one must not remain
dangling,
as you are, hanged one! —

Oh, Zarathustra,
most cruel Nimrod!
till now ever God's huntsman
the snare-net of all virtues,
the arrow of the evil ones!
Now —
hunted down by your self,
your own prey,
gnawing into yourself...
Now

at one with yourself,
twosome in your own knowledge
among a hundred mirrors
but false to yourself,
among a hundred
memories
uncertain,
weary at every wound,
cold with every frost,
strangled by one's own ropes,
<u>Self-knower</u>!
<u>Self-hangman</u>!

Why did you constrict yourself
with the ropes of your
wisdom?
Why did you entice yourself
into the paradise of the old
serpent?
Why did you sneak
into <u>your</u> <u>self</u> — into <u>your</u> <u>self</u>?

Now sick,
made ill by
snake poison;
a prisoner now
who drew the hardest lot:
in your own well-shaft,

bowed while working,
entrapped in yourself,
digging at yourself,
clumsy,
stiff,
a corpse
overwhelmed by hundreds of
burdens,
overburdened by yourself,
a <u>knower</u>!
a <u>self-knower</u>!
the <u>wise</u> Zarathustra!...

You sought the heaviest burden:
and so, you found <u>yourself</u> —
you cannot cast loose from <u>yourself</u>...

Lying in wait,
cowering,
one who no longer
stands upright!
You misshape things
for me with
your grave, you <u>malformed</u> spirit!...

Earlier you were ever so proud
on all the stilts of your
pride!

Earlier you were a hermit
without God
and a twin-partner of the
devil,
the scarlet prince of
arrogance!...

Now —
warped
between two nothings
a question mark,
a tired riddle —
a riddle for <u>birds of prey</u> ...

- - they will "solve" you,
surely,
they hunger for your
"resolution,"
already they flutter around
you, their riddle,
around you, hanged one!...
Oh, Zarathustra!
<u>Self-knower</u>!
<u>Self-hangman</u>!

                           Translated by Siegfried Mandel from German

THE POET FIRDUSI
(Goldne Menschen, Silbermenschen)

HEINRICH HEINE

Heinrich Heine, the German lyric and satiric poet, was born of Jewish parents in Dusseldorf. In 1825, to be granted his law degree from Gottingen University, he nominally became a Protestant. Six years later he chose self-exile in revolutionary, culturally advanced Paris, where he died in 1856. Toward the end of his life Heine was bedridden, victim of an illness that left him paralyzed; but during that time he produced some of his most extraordinary work.

The subject of this poem, Firdusi, was born about 940 a.d., and became one of the first major Islamic poets. His fortune exhausted by his commitment to his art, he sought help from Sultan Mahmud, ruler of the Ghaznavid Empire, centered in Afghanistan. Firdusi, however, died a poor man in 1020. His epic **SHAH NAMAH**, *in 60,000 verses, is the first great work of modern Persian literature.*

A <u>toman</u> is a Persian coin; those minted of gold have great value; those of silver are relatively worthless.

1.
Golden people, silver people!
A toman, when some poor rascal
mentions it, is only silver.
Silver's the toman he thinks of.

On a sovereign's tongue, however,
a toman is always golden.
Nothing but a gold toman
does a shah accept or offer.

That's how good folk understand it,
and Firdusi thought so too,
author of the celebrated,
awe-inspiring work, "Shah Namah."

He created this great epic
under orders of the Shah,
who had promised him beforehand
a toman for every verse.

Ten and seven times the rose bloomed,
ten and seven times she withered,
ten and seven times the nightin-
gale extolled her and fell silent.

During all this while the poet
sat before the loom of fancy
day and night, and diligently
wove his song's enormous carpet —

giant carpet — and the poet
marvelously wove within it
fabled records of his homeland:
Farsistan's primeval monarchs,

favorite heroes of his people,
knightly exploits, grand adventures,
sprites of witchery, and demons,
boldly twined with legend-blossoms:

everything in bloom and vibrant,
rich with color, glowing, blazing,
beamed upon as though from heaven

by the blest Iranian radiance,

by the ancient light, divinely
pure, whose final fire temple,
spite of the Koran and mufti,
blazed within the poet's heart.

When the epic was completed,
its creator sent his patron
the entire manuscript
twice a hundred thousand verses.

It was in the bathing room,
in the bathing room of Gasna,
that the Shah's black messengers
came upon the great Firdusi.

Each one dragged a bag of money,
knelt, and placed it at the feet
of the poet, as high payment
for his masterly achievement.

Hastily the bard tore open
both full bags, to drink refreshment
from the sight of gold — long pined for;
but he saw, with consternation,

that these bags had only silver —
pale tomans, tomans of silver —
roughly twice a hundred thousand —
and the bard laughed bitterly.

Laughing bitterly he piled
his award in equal portions,

and to each of the two black
messengers he gave one-third

as imbursement for his service,
and the last third he presented
to a bath-slave, who'd attended
on his bath, as drinking money.

Now he seized his wander-staff,
left the capital behind him:
but outside the gate Firdusi
shook the vile dust from his shoes.

2.
"Had he failed to keep his vow,
as men do, and merely broken
what was pledged, the word he'd spoken,
I would not be angry now.

"But unpardonably vile
that he cheated me by scheming:
by his speech of double meaning
and, still worse, by silent guile.

"He was stately, grand of limb,
noble in his every air;
few alive that could compare
kingly — every inch of him.

"Like a sunrise in the sky,
eyes aflame he looked at me,
model of integrity —
yet he snared me with a lie."

3.
The Shah has revelled in his food,
and now he's in a mellow mood.

He sits at dusk by a purple pool
beside a fountain. It ripples so cool!

His servants lean with a reverent air;
Ansari, his favorite, is there.

Blooming from many a marble urn
swarms of flowers gorgeously burn.

Gracefully, each an odalisque,
the palm trees fan themselves in the dusk.

Motionless, every cypress stands
won from this world, in a heavenly trance.

But lo! at the lute's delicious word
a soft, mysterious song is heard.

The Shah starts up like a man possessed:
"Who is the author of this text?"

Ansari, whom he was questioning, spoke:
"This is a poem Firdusi wrote."

"Firdusi?" cried the monarch: "How
_is_ the great bard? Where is he now?"

Ansari answered: "In hunger and tears
he has been struggling for many years

"in Thus, the city that gave him birth;
there he gardens a poor bit of earth."

The Shah fell silent; then he decreed:
"Ansari, these orders require speed —

"Go to my stables and choose with care
a hundred mules, the sturdiest there,

"and fifty camels; load them with treasure
such as will lift a heart with pleasure:

"splendors and wonders, expensive wear
and fine utensils, graceful and rare,
"of sandalwood, ivory — sweet to behold;
marvelous pipes of silver and gold,

"craftily handled cups and pots,
leopard-skins with spectacular spots,

"carpets and shawls and rich brocade
which artisans of my lands have made —

"along with these, you must not fail
to load bright arms and brighter mail,

"and every drink that could come to mind,
preserves as well, of every kind,

"candies and gingerbreads galore
and almond-pastries by the score,

"twelve horses of Arabian breed
— swift as an arrow, every steed,

"and twelve black slaves with bodies of brass
impervious to all duress.

"Ansari, gather this grand array

and start on your journey right away.

"Bring my best wishes with everything else
to Thus, where the great Firdusi dwells."

Ansari obeyed the charge of the crown;
she loaded the mules and camels down

with gifts of tribute, for which he had spent
what a whole province pays in rent.

Three days later, the Persian prince
departed from his residence

and rode in person at their head
under his royal banner of red.

They reached Thus after an eight-day ride;
the city rests at a mountain's side.

Through the west gate, with a jubilant din,
the Shah and his caravan came in.

The bugler burst, the drummer pounded,
a song of celebration sounded.

"Allah be praised!" from lusty throat
the cheers of the camel-drivers broke.

But at that very instant, through
the east gate of the town withdrew

a slow cortege that bore the dead
Firdusi to his final bed.

TRANSLATED BY AARON KRAMER FROM GERMAN

ICARUS

Philippe Desportes

Philippe Desportes charmed the courts of Renaissance France with his clever, suave poetry. He frequently penned for others the verse they felt inadequate to create. ICARUS *was the liminal poem in* AMOURS D'HIPPOLYTE, *a collection of poetry written for Marguerite of Valois at the request of a gentleman.*

Here fell young Icarus, who dared to try
    To seek that heaven with wings, courageous fell
All noble hearts with longing so to die.
O happy deed, whose trivial penalty
    His glorious spirit hath rewarded well!
    O happy woe, full of such good! I tell
Of centuries conquered, victim's victory.

His youth shunned not a road so fresh as this.
The power he lacked, but the attempt was his
    The fairest star sufficed to burn the brave.
His death befell him in high enterprise;
He sought the sky, and in the sea he lies.
Is there a fairer wish, a finer grave?

Translated by Charles Plumb from French

SLAUGHTERED VILLAGE

Salem Jubran

Salem Jubran was born in 1941 in the Gallilee. A graduate of the Haifa University with degrees in English literature and Medieval history, he has published three books of poetry, **WORDS FROM THE HEART, UNRESTRICTED POEMS, *and* BROTHER OF SUN.** *His work has been translated into English, French, Russian, Finnish, Spanish, Chinese, Japanese and Hebrew. His poetry is both realistic and romantic; he is regarded as one of the most important living Palestinian poets.*

Blood   blood   blood
As if the earth would not grow grass without blood
Flesh on top of flesh
The destruction arouses the wild beast's appetite
for destruction

The children wander to and fro
between the fire and the storm-whirled dust
as if the black ruins had cut off their mother' breasts
before their eyes
They whisper "water!"
Who is to give it to you children?
The sky?
Even the dove has flown away from this hell
Even the dove...

Translated by W. M. Barzelay from Arabic

PALESTINIAN BOY

W. M. Barzelay

Born in 1924, Walter M. Barzelay remains one of Israel's most widely translated poets, having been published in Arabic, Italian, Japanese, Portuguese, Russian, and Swedish among other languages. The recipient of awards and medals for his own translations, Barzelay is the Hebrew translator of **SELECTED VERSE** *by N. Guillen. He died in 1987 in a sanitorium near Moscow. The following contribution was selected by his widow, Rina Barzelay, of Tel Aviv.*

Just on the day

I had become fifteen

they shot me

in the light of midday

They buried me

wrapped in the dark of night

In my mother's pupils

the light of wind-beaten torches

fluttered in the dance of Death

Between my father's eyelids

and between the lids of my brothers

the echoes of the fire were ablaze

They shot me

because of my crime

of not bowing my head

to the masters

For that they shot me

But one day I'll arise

in the light of day I'll rise

and hurl my fifteen years

like stones

into the faces of those

who shot me.

Translated by W. M. Barzelay from Hebrew

CHILDREN

Yosef Sharon

Yosef Sharon was born in 1952. His two books of poetry are **SPEECH** *and* **A PERIOD IN A CITY**. *A third book is due to be published soon. He has also written about architecture in Israel. Sharon lives in Tel Aviv.*

To pee and to hide,

to go underground, showing off the new quartz watch,

or measuring the length of sexual organs with a ruler.

Escaping from the more tended, close environment

they come here to the scaffolding

of the residential building

going up by the beach road, after Ramat Aviv.

The graffiti: "Begin, get out of Lebanon"

smeared on one of the unplastered walls,

still written there and already beyond grasp

as if covered with some dust from past generations.

Running, and when they get tired of circling the wall

that surrounds the yard -

they burst forth into the open field,

and their eyes seem to go out of their sockets to the yellow

nothingness: sunflowers.

Nervous eyes, not a gentle spark of life.

And one lifts a stone, feels it,

turning into a soft cap in his hand,

and in his nervousness is a certain guiding line:

he shoots it at once, forming an arc.

And the temptation to hit, too, and the bad prayer

when failing to get out of the circle surrounding you:

here is the apple not far from the tree,

here is the house that is always nearby,

here is the advantage of its being here,

and suddenly this advantage irritates.

But while you bind a scarf around your neck

out of some habit of self-abasement and love-of-a-cold

(so the scarf becomes vital, of course),

they've already climbed a mound

facing the sea, simply standing and watching.

You, like a fish in a transparent fishnet, and they

already know it's possible just to look at the sea,

just like that, not to strain the eyes.

                          TRANSLATED BY LINDA ZISQUIT FROM HEBREW

FROM A CHILDHOOD

Rainer Maria Rilke

Rainer Marie Rilke was born in 1875 in Prague, and moved to Paris in 1902. He was deeply influenced by his friendship with the French sculptor Auguste Rodin. The spiritual vision of his poetry continues to capture the imagination of modern readers.

The darkness was like riches in the room

where the boy sat hidden.

And when his mother entered, as in a dream

a glass shivered in a silent cupboard.

She felt that the room betrayed her

and kissed her son: Are you there?...

Then both looked anxiously at the piano,

for on many evenings she played a song

in which the child felt strangely caught.

He sat very still. His wide gaze clung

to her hand, bent with many rings,

as if it went heavily through

snowdrifts over the white keys.

Translated by Vern Rutsala from German

JOSEPH'S SUSPICION

Rainer Maria Rilke

And the angel spoke and was patient
with the man who was clenching his fists:
But don't you see in every fold
she's as fresh as God's early morning?

But the man, gazing at him darkly,
only mumbled: What has changed her so?
But at this the angel cried: Carpenter,
do you still not see the Lord God is acting?

Because you make boards, do you,
in your pride, take Him to task
who modestly from the same wood
makes buds swell and leaves appear?

He understood. And as he, frightened,
raised his eyes to the angel,
it was gone. He slowly pulled off
his thick cap. And he sang praise.

Translated by Norbert Krapf from German

(#286) ABOUT STALIN

OSIP MANDEL'SHTAM

The Russian poet, Osip Mandel'shtam, was, with Anna Akhmatova and Nikolai Gumilov, a leading member of the avant-garde Acmeist movement in the Soviet Union. The circumstances of his death in 1938 remain controversial.

We live without feeling a country beneath us;
Ten paces away, unheard are our speeches;

But where we catch half a discourse,
The Kremlin mountaineer's discussed.

His thick fingers are as greasy as worms,
but there's truth like forty-pound weights in his words.

Laughing cockroaches—a moustache—
And a great shine from his topboots.

And around him a mob of thin-necked chieftains—
He toys with the services of half-persons.

They whistle, they whimper, they mew;
He alone merely rams and pokes.

Like horseshoes he forges decree on decree—
In your groin or your forehead, your brow or your eye.

Death sentences taste like citrons
To the broad-chested Ossetian.

(November 1933)

TRANSLATED BY PAUL T. HOPPER FROM RUSSIAN

THE MADMAN

S. J. Pretorius

S. J. Pretorius, born in Postmasburg, Transvaal, South Africa, taught for many years at the University of South Africa. A recurrent theme of his poetry concerns the Afrikaner leaving farm and small town life and adjusting to the modern urban city. He has published six volumes of poetry, the first one, **VONKE (SPARKS)**, *in 1943.*

In this body

underneath the skin

and the surfaces of the eye

two of us dwell

a madman

and me

The madman groans

shrieks

I remain silent

afraid

Each night

as we fight each other

in this cramped space

I become more worn down

He wins

hurling screams

at God

his fury

at the world

and me

In this country

of flesh and bone

two of us inhabit

One of us is insane

I am the other

                    Translated by John Brander from Afrikaans

DIARY
(THE LAST THOUGHTS OF KAFKA'S SISTER BEFORE BEING GASSED)

ADRIAN PAUNESCU

Adrian Paunescu, a recognized poet in Romania, received that country's Writers Union Award in 1968. In 1970, he was poet-in-residence at the International Writing Program at the University of Iowa.

One by one we suffer the questioning,
The cat's claws scratch at our backs.
When we writhe, when we choke with terror,
When our hearts pound like high-boot heels
Before the goose-step and the trouser braid..

We are mice, we are grade-A mice,
We have so many needs and flaws:
We like to breathe and run about,
We like a cellar well-furnished.
We've learned to live with the cat's laws.

And from time to time, we're summoned, questioned:
"What's the trouble? What's got into you?
The cat's paws are well manicured."
Mute as a monument,
Facing our graves like a sphinx.

TRANSLATED BY EVA FEILER & STANLEY H. BARKAN FROM ROMANIAN

ULYSSES

Umberto Saba

Umberto Saba was born in Trieste in 1883 and died in Gorizia in 1957. As a young man, he worked for a business firm in Trieste, but soon gave it up to devote himself to poetry. After World War I, he opened an antiquarian bookstore in Trieste, but, as a Jew, was forced to flee to France and later to Florence (where he was sheltered by Eugenio Montale) to escape persecution under the increasingly oppressive Fascist racial laws. In 1946 he won the Viareggio Prize for poetry, and in 1951 that of the Accademia dei Lincei.

I sailed my ship along Dalmatian shores

in my youth. From the waves jagged islets

jutted, emeralds flashing in the sun,

seaweed-slippery, where seldom a seabird

paused, intent on prey. To flee their treachery,

when darkness and the flood tide drowned them, ships

drifting leeward would come about to touch

the wind. Today my kingdom is that land

of No-man. Lights in the harbor beckon

to others, but I steer for the open sea,

spurred by a restless spirit as of old,

and by a love, with sorrow strewn, of life.

TRANSLATED BY ELIO ZAPPULLA FROM ITALIAN

From UNDER THE INFLUENCE OF THE MANDOLIN

Zalman Schne'or

A tireless traveler, Zalman Schne'or left his home in Shklov, Byelorussia, at the age of 13. After living in Warsaw and Paris, he took an extended tour through Europe and North Africa. "To the Strains of the Mandolin," the cycle of poems from which this excerpt is taken, examines the poet's relationship to the non-Jewish world he lives in. Schne'or settled in Israel in 1951, where he is buried there alongside Saul Tchernikowsky and Hayyim Bialik, two other great figures of Hebrew poetry of Schne'or's generation.

I am a prince in exile ——

look at my wandering shoes, embroidered with silver

how old and torn they are,

look at the elegant darkened skin on my cheeks,

inheritance of the East that will never fade away.

How deep is the contempt and sorrow in my eyes.

All the seas have sunk into my depth,

all the tears are contained in my tear,

all the rivers of agony fall into my sea,

and my sea is never full.

In the baggage of my wandering are many documents of my roots,

no king can boast their match:

the debts of many nations

upon their victories

upon their wealth and greatness

upon their pride and

upon the glories of their kingdoms.

All these are written with blood and with the tears of
      forefathers.

God in his majesty signed them,

attested by Moses, his scribe;

and the witnesses are your messiah, the prophet of Arabia,

and all the prophets of God, are witnesses.

In spite of all this, nations renounce me,

the Jew, a wretched nobleman without a sword.

Their spiritual attributes, their worldly wealth and their power,

together with the treasures of my soul, they copied

in the names of different gods, the names of different saints

as do many sons without names

and many thieves;

they enrich themselves on borrowed gains.

And now the whole world belongs to them

in all its beauty and its glory —

to them belong the cries of the battles,

the happy laughter of peace,

the tears of those who sow the land

and the songs of the vintners.

To them belong the anger of the fire,

the dreams of the builders.

And I, a stepson to the land, forgotten nobleman,

how will I claim my property?

How will I redeem the treasures of my soul?

Along the twisted path, on every main highway,

I sought my faith,

I knocked on every gate of justice that I saw

And no one would return to me my looted soul.

None will redeem my debts. . . .

. . . All my wandering is an eternal mirror of their wickedness.

I am the stain of Cain on the forehead of all nations,

a mean stain of blood on the justice of the heart of the world,

a deep stain, very deep, that they cannot erase

with fire, with blood, or with unceasing waters.

For who did not contrive

to erase my name from the dark history of hidden sins?

And who is the one who refused to burn the scrolls of my last debts and to plunder the dearest remnants from my sack?

Every ignorant, every simpleton, and wicked man,

every barbarian who has left his forest and the skins of wolves

came out into the open

to warm himself in the glow of my light

and to burn his obscurity in my fire.

And this decadent land still flatters them

by adorning itself with green grass fresh every spring

and with light, white foam on its beaches.

It whispers from the golden fields

"I am your mother."

And sings with joy from the waterfalls

and lovingly looks at them from blue rivers.

TRANSLATED BY ABRAHAM ALMANY FROM HEBREW

THE CRITIC

Johann Wolfgang von Goethe

Johann Wolfgang von Goethe (1749-1832) is considered to be the most broadly influential of all German writers. His importance in the history of poetry, the novel and drama is legendary, and his critical writing did much to spread Romanticism throughout Western Europe.

The bastard even came to dinner.

I didn't mind his company.

I ate what I usually eat.

He stuffed himself with everything

And drank himself under the table.

When he felt he was full enough

Damn if he didn't visit my neighbor,

Where the stupid fool tried to complain

The soup didn't have enough seasoning,

The meat was too rare, and the wine sour.

What do you do with an idiot like that?

Kill him. Disguised as a critic.

Translated by James Schevill from German

EPITAPH

                                                                  EUGENE SCRIBE

Eugene Scribe, the nineteenth century French dramatist, is generally credited with reviving public taste for vaudeville. He eventually developed the <u>comedie-vaudeville</u>, a comedy that combines drama and music.

In life my librettos, plays by the score,

Created friends for me, money, fame.

After such a happy life, in Heaven <u>Encore</u>!

                                                     TRANSLATED BY JAMES SCHEVILL FROM FRENCH

UNTITLED

Pir Sultan Abdal

Little is known of Pir Sultan Abdal, except that he lived in Eastern Turkey during the late seventeenth century upheavals known as the Jelali Rebellions. His songs are passionate calls to revolution couched in Shi'A Muslim language of sacrifice and redemption.

I too have come into this world to live

Let my case rest, in the hands of the Court

Muhammad and Ali are my counsel

Let my case rest, in the hands of the Court

Those who must tire, let them do so, I will never tire out

I will never leave the abode of the dervishes

I am not answerable before the judge of this world

Let my case rest, in the hands of the Court

I gave power of attorney to God the Creator

Can He be an oppressor like His creatures?

There they make men confess, one by one

Let my case rest, in the hands of the Court

The believer, the Muslim falls and is gathered up

The broken and the wounded are cured

Earth and stone melt into pure thin air

Let my case rest, in the hands of the Court

O Pir Sultan Abdal: This world is a hive

They go out as the just rulers; they come back the brethren

The court of Muhammad is a mighty court

Let my case rest, in the hands of the Court

TRANSLATED BY P. N. REMLER FROM TURKISH

A Variation on Catullus's ODI ET AMO

GAIUS VALERIUS CATULLUS

A Roman poet who lived during the time of Julius Caesar, Gaius Valerius Catullus left over 100 poems. Many seem to be more like fragments, and most of them are quite short. They surge with emotion, and have provided models of love poetry for Edmund Spenser and Ben Jonson.

I hate and I love: you sentimentalists, don't ask me why - -

Love's cruelty is celebrated in every lost, sunlit eye.

TRANSLATED BY JAMES SCHEVILL FROM LATIN

OAKS AND ROSES

Sarah Kirsch

Sarah Kirsch, whose writing has been awarded several prizes in Germany, Austria, and Italy, was born in 1935 in Limlingerode, Germany. After studying biology, she turned to the study of literature. In 1977, she took up residence in former West Berlin, and now lives in northern Germany, not far from the Danish border.

I've bought myself a timetable in Ferlinghetti's

Store and I sit in the Pullman car

And ride along the coast day and night and the poet

Mirrors his cowhead in the window we ride

Endlessly into Wyoming line by line man

Oh man what a pace and I see him with an

Astrakhan cap in a tinplate village the tottering

Telegraph poles are just about toppling and the highway

Cruisers howl like wolves, on a crossing.

The world is a farmstead in winter we can't

Get in fog flies when I go to the window

And the magnificent trees in Germany

Hike by fiery as American oaks

Roses rot in Presbyterian graveyards

And his poem keeps cracking track-jolts

Wicked wicked talk abstruse rooks

And when it has gotten extremely dark and we find ourselves

Unbounded steppe in our view white heather

On the Transcyrillian Railway, come

Into the open friend and we spell live backwards

Ask what can have become of the wild boys Yevgeny Andrei

In the meantime and we fly

Through the boundless untappable birchwoods of the Czar

Lev Kopelev waves to us a track-layer

With a bag of black earth from home his giant head

White beard accompany us long can't be

Wiped off the pane before the beautiful wagon

Drives up in autumnal fiery flames.

TRANSLATED FROM GERMAN BY CHARLES FISHMAN & MARINA ROSCHER

WINTER'S END

Dan Pagis

Dan Pagis was born in Bukovina in 1930, and survived his imprisonment in a concentration camp during World War II. He emigrated to Israel, where he became professor of medieval Hebrew literature at the Hebrew University of Jerusalem, and one of the major poets of his generation. Among the several books of his poetry translated into English is **POINTS OF DEPARTURE**. *Stephen Mitchell is the translator of this volume.*

Good snowman,
your coal eyes envision blackness,
only blackness. How much courage
is reflected in your eyes.
Not a single blink. In the center,
your nose still protrudes a little,
that pessimistic carrot.
Rejoice, my friend, in your old age.
It's true that you and I at winter's end
are somewhat less substantial than we were,
but you know just as well as I
your winter days like mine were beautiful,
and beautiful will be our summer.
Why are we waiting for it in the back yard?
Let us steal away from here right now
before the spring mud, and course
swiftly and light-heartedly
down the sloping road and onward
toward the wide sea—if it really exists.
Tomorrow the radio will announce
that no trace of us
will ever be found.

Translated from Hebrew by Robert Friend & Shimon Sandbank

REQUIEM FOR THE MISSING

Victor Manuel Rivera Toledo

Victor Manuel Rivera Toledo was born in Castenengo, Guatemala in 1907. He was appointed to the Consulate of Guatemala in New York City before serving as a member of the Guatemalan Delegation to the United Nations. He served in this capacity until his death in 1984.

The dead do not care for their names,
nor for a cross
or a tombstone
so they may read their epitaphs.

Only the living care for that,
those who stay behind, crying:
the mothers
the widows
the orphans
who do not know where their dead are.

The dead are important to those who wait
in vain and suspect the worst;
the living wish for the return
of those who disappeared without a trace,
for their return so they can be surrounded by light,
so they can be near the warmth.

If only the dead were dead,
if only the living could have them, though they are lifeless:
to lay them in the earth

and at least to see their eyes,
though closed;

to see their faces, no matter
that the flesh is painted with death.

The missing, the nameless,
the dead in a watery grave, covered with mud.
The dead, thrown into rivers
by human animals who contaminate the
elements with the decay of bloody faces of the dead.

Others, abandoned in cemeteries
without crosses, clandestine cemeteries,
where no one goes for fear of the dogs.

The rivers are not crystal clear anymore;
the rivers are no longer white.
The surf is not white, but blood-red.

The ships of death sail in the rivers;
the rivers are liquid coffins
that carry the dead to the sea,
an immense burial for the fallen;
for the missing men
a blue burial without crosses,
without epitaphs.
The waves recite a requiem for the missing.

TRANSLATED BY LUIS EDUARDO RIVERA FROM SPANISH

I AM BLACK

Rado

Rado is the pen name of Celestin Andriamanantena. Jerome Brooks and Raymond Patterson are translating and publishing a collection of his poetry.

I am black

But I am far from defeated!

On the contrary, I am proud of this blackness,

The color of burning coals.

Not the sunlight alone shines,

Among the good things seen on this earth,

But the very darkest pitch-black night

Embracing the distant stars.

Thank God for the night!

Thank God for blackness!

Thank God I am black!

Grow blacker, my skin!

Accept a blackness the color of burning coals.

The sun makes fertile the land.

Blackness brings forth heroes to startle the world.

Translated by Jerome Brooks & Raymond Patterson from Malagasy

ON MY STREET

Fado Song by N.Campos & M.L.Barbosa

Full of melancholy and <u>saudade</u> (a deep longing), the Fado (meaning <u>fate</u>) folk music of Portugal is rich in tradition. Originating in the Lisbon and Coimbra areas as an urban folk song, the poorer people chanted of the cruelty of fate, suffering, and death. The <u>fadista</u> (singer of Fado) expresses in song his/her heartfelt passion and misery. A viola and guitar traditionally accompany the <u>fadista</u>. The stringed instruments carry the beat which is melancholic and deeply moving. The lyrics are simple and to the point. Most often the song speaks of honest love, lost or found, usually of love unrequited. Occasionally the Fado is of a positive nature, as in the case of "On My Street." This "happy" type of Fado is less common and not characteristic of the genre.

On my street

there is a simple house

with a door and a window

in the shape of a heart.

And when the full moon

shines upon the facade

it is illuminated

as if it were a star.

On my street

night or day

happiness reigns

in this modest house.

On my street
just around the corner
in this small house
it is always a day of celebration.

Come close and see
how all who live there are happy.
You can be sure
anytime you arrive will be the best time.

If you are my friend
don't hesitate to enter
for in this home
there will always be room
for one more.

TRANSLATED BY CARLOS & RHONDA CUNHA FROM PORTUGUESE

SAVEZ-VOUS PLANTER LES CHOUX?

French Children's Song

As a poem, this children's song is rewritten with the singer's body each time it is properly recited.

Tell me, tell me, tell me how
You plant a cabbage, plant a cabbage.
Tell me, tell me, tell me how
You plant a cabbage in the ground?

1.
First you plant it with your hands,
And you press it down, you press it.
This is how you press it down,
As you plant it in the ground.

2.
Then you stamp it with your foot,
And you stamp it down, you stamp it.
Then you stamp it all around,
As you plant it in the ground.

3.
Then you smell it with your nose,
And you sniff it and you smell it,
Then you sniff it all around,
As you plant it in the ground.

__4__.
Then you roll it with your back,
Turning here and all around,
Then you roll and roll about,
As you plant it in the ground.

__5__.
Then you touch it with your head,
Nodding up and nodding down.
Then you touch it with your head,
and now you have your cabbage bed!

Translated by Ruth Rubin from French

SNOW

H. Leivick

H. Leivick was born in the small town of Igumen in Byelorussia in 1888. As a young man, he was arrested a number of times for socialist activities. In 1912, he was sentenced to life imprisonment in Siberia. Somehow he managed to escape, and came to America in 1914. Here he became a poet and playwright. He died in 1962.

We sit at a small table

over a glass of tea

and behind the windows

the snow is falling.

We are silent.

The words lie breathing

on the table.

The words tremble

like fish newly caught.

Don't the words see the snow?

The snow falling

behind the windows.

Translated by Harold Black from Yiddish

THIS IS YOU

JOHANNES EDFELT

Johannes Edfelt (b. 1904) is a poet, translator, and essayist, who has enjoyed a long and distinguished literary career. Since 1968 he has been a member of the Swedish Academy and served on its Nobel Committee (1974-1989). **EKOLODNING (ECHO SOUNDING**, *1986) a collection of his poetry written over a period of 60 years, ran to 12,000 copies. He has produced 22 volumes of translations. Camden House recently published Edfelt's* **SELECTED POEMS**, *translated by W. H. Auden, Robin Fulton, David Ignatow, Stephen Klass, George C. Schoolfield, Leif Sjoberg and William Jay Smith.*

The numbing accumulation of forms in Indian art I understand better at the sight of the street life of the people, which is part of its background. At the outskirts of Agra, I encounter in the space of only a few hundred yards a snake-charmer who on an upraised arm carries a cobra, of course without its sting; four cripples shuffling along in the country-road dust; a crowd of men and women carrying large bundles of twigs on their heads and children gathering camel's droppings underneath the tamarind trees by the wayside, all filled with emerald green parrots. In the middle of the throng of bicycle rickshaws and handcarts the cows, the holy cows, roam about with complete unconcern. The only surprising thing is that on this stretch of road one does not meet anyone on stilts, nor anyone who is leading a bear on a jingling chain.

TRANSLATED BY DAVID IGNATOW & LEIF SJOBERG FROM SWEDISH

PORTENTS

FOLKE ISAKSSON

Folke Isaksson, born in 1927 in Kalix, Sweden, had his **COLLECTED POEMS** *published in 1988. He has translated Wallace Stevens (1957), Blake's* **MARRIAGE OF HEAVEN AND HELL** *(1988) and more recently two volumes of the Hungarian poet Sandor Csoori into Swedish.*

All of a sudden the crust of the earth feels so thin, the fire underneath so close. The entire foundation which had been built up with such labor totters. The vibrations in the exterior are transmitted to the interior. There is a hard wind blowing, as before a huge storm. The cold and slow animals make their way up from their burrows, and the swallow's compass-needle quivers over the splintered mirror of the water.

Omens appear, communications with texts hard to interpret. In the wet sand the migrating birds have signed their letters of farewell. Words which will be effaced by the wave, so that only individual letters remain, messages the sea throws back with a dull mumble.

Something moves beneath the dark trees. In a cellar-black glade, light flames up, shadows flutter. In the dawn light, when the wonder-working night jar hides its head under its wing, one can discern traces, a faintly gleaming ring, in the tall grass. It looks like the amorous hedgehogs' beaten track, which goes around, around amid fescue and orchard grass, the obstinate movement, the persistent urge, the wisdom of cells.

Portents and strangled cries. A harsh glare floods the speckled bird's egg with light, a reddish scallop casts about inside the shell, a movement which breaks off at the tough membrane. The loom knocks more heavily, more convulsively. Missed knots show up in the webbing, hollows and dropped stitches disrupt the pattern, and the spider which had listened in its shady corner for the piercing command goes astray among its filaments.

Someone who puts his ear to the ground hears a faint clatter. Whatever is exposed is unable to conceal its fragility. The brownie scout cannot hide in her own shadow. The lizard cannot dart out of the way and give his tail in pledge. The fox comes up to my house and observes me questioningly. When I cannot give any answer, it turns and leaves behind a fume of the wild.

The ocean breathes. The seals climb up to the surface and observe the people. They look at them with their dark eyes, with eyes heavy with darkness. The lighted darkness down in their element has become turbid, its life is dissolved into new substances, the primordial ooze is changed to muck, it wells in along the beaches and soils the rock.

Once, when the earth was young, they lay about on the outermost skerries. The combers that played over the islets, the gentle rocking in the tidal pools, the playfulness of the glitter, the conversation. Their indolent bodies and, farthest away in the corner of their eye a tiny point, the craft in which two fur-clad men were paddling. The pulse of the chase, the song of the sirens and the sooty kettle over the fire, in a cleft in the rock at the water's edge.

TRANSLATED BY STEPHEN KLASS & LEIF SJOBERG FROM SWEDISH

I'D LOVE TO LOVE LOVING

FERNANDO PESSOA

Fernando Antonio Nogueira Pessoa was born in Lisbon, Portugal in 1888, but spent his childhood in South Africa, where his stepfather was Portuguese consul. A complicated figure, Pessoa is associated with a literary trend known as <u>saudosismo</u>, a blend of pantheistic and nostalgic elements that yielded a form of mystical nationalism. The poet died in 1935.

I'd love to love loving.

Just a minute...reach me a cigarette

from that pack on the bedside table.

Go on...you were saying that

as metaphysics developed

from Kant to Hegel

something got lost.

I agree totally.

I was listening, really.

<u>Nondum amabam et amare amabam</u> (St. Augustine)

Such a curious business, this association of ideas!

I'm so sick of thinking about feeling something else!

Thanks. Let me light up. Go ahead. Hegel...

TRANSLATED BY EDWIN HONIG FROM PORTUGUESE

BALLAD OF HRDLICKA'S WITCH

Frederick Brainin

Frederick Brainin, who publishes in German under the name of Fritz Brainin, is a native of Vienna, and is known as a poet and translator. He lives in New York City.

I

Where videos pain you, Schwechat airport witch

frail under your poncho, with their rock hard rain,

where only Pluto's police dogs trace your itch

for heavenly white snow (translation: cocaine!)

there through the gate for my poor soul's x-ray

I'll fly our trip on tape to JFK.

II

When sharply drops away the Waldheimat prone

as Swissair's pilot sounds the speedup claxon

(what strange stewardess put on ear's phone

your Lenya's Pirate Jenny sung by La Jackson?)

then, deaf-mute blind passenger, I lose

your Hrdlicka nude model's streetwasher blues.

III

Wasn't your pact (with Muriel Gardner's [1] press

in the Vienna woods!) T. Kramer's [2] freedom to guard?

You, Irma Trksak, shot code spy in the SS,

Irina Ratushinskaya [3] at her mad ward?

Now like the goddess after Tiananmen Square's death

your stowaway's antipollution mask filters your breath:

L'envoi

A U-bahn farebeater back in New York City

I've found you, subway panhandler, hooked on jazz,

to sell your Vindobona cave graffiti ...

What remains: the translator's loneliness.

TRANSLATED BY FREDERICK BRAININ FROM GERMAN

[1] American journalist in anti-Nazi underground
[2] Viennese poet in wartime English exile
[3] "My mouse and I
  will invent a land,
  where there are neither
  cats nor camps." (I.R.)

SONG IN A DEAD LANGUAGE

Nikolai Kantchev

Nikolai Kantchev is one of Bulgaria's leading poets. Author of several books of poetry, he is widely translated, and is represented in all English-language collections of Bulgarian poetry. He resides in Sofia, Bulgaria.

The melonstems strain forward to see

their lives measured by a summer's span.

They lose track of time as the season passes,

seeing only short-necked wolves, those who cease to exist.

Well, aren't we all remnants? A melonstem's not a rope.

Yet the word that sticks beneath the knot in our throats,

isn't that the answer we've been waiting for?

The eagle atop the sky becomes the symbol

of his own power. But what am I,

the one from the valley? The one who sends

thousands of messages by passing birds to dead kings,

reminding me with their desert-dry forms:

What wonders spring from the dew of Egypt.

Oh, my tears remain helpless,

while I cry inside a crocodile's skin.

If I wear my shepherd's coat once more,

will these lumps of torment speak

for the dust scattered through all the ages?

Have the Aztecs said something for my time

with words of corn and the Assyrians

in their dead rooster's cackle? Oh, history,

you're chanting this as a lullaby

but the choir of gnats revives the tale of my call.

TRANSLATED BY BRADLEY R. STRAHAN & PAMELA PERRY FROM BULGARIAN

THE SECONDS

Hirsh Osherovitch

Hirsh Osherovitch was born in Lithuania in 1908. His first volume of poems was published in 1941. In 1949 he was arrested for Zionist activities and served seven years in Soviet labor camps. In 1971 he emigrated to Israel, where he has published nine volumes of verse. He has been awarded numerous literary prizes.

Wait! Wait! Wait! Wait!
the seconds say and escape.
I hate their rush to go
as though they were running out
to sell me piece by piece.

Wait! Wait! Wait! Wait!
Wait for whom or what?
Do they ever do their own bidding?
Crying Wait! as they skid

into the pit to be forgotten
and never come back.
A mirage, a mirage from the start
that you thought in your heart
of building an eternity out of not-becoming.

From <u>Gezang in Labyrint</u>, Tel Aviv, 1977

Translated by Seymour Levitan from Yiddish

UPROOTED

JACOB STERNBERG

Jacob Sternberg was born in the region known as Bessarabia in 1890. His first volume of verse was published in 1935. In 1948, he was sentenced to five years in a Siberian labor camp. In 1965, he was acclaimed in Moscow as a major Soviet Yiddish writer.

What will I lean on
(besides the pride of my bitter old age)
when I am gathered
to my fathers?

Empty of belief and disbelief,
a lightless window staring at the night.

Having never done good or sinned,
childless, friendless, and without kin.

I have no people of my own, no witness—
is it precisely this that constitutes my binding?

In this century, harsh and cold as ice,
you live naked and you die naked.

From <u>Di Goldene Keyt</u>, No. 92, 1977

TRANSLATED BY SEYMOUR LEVITAN FROM YIDDISH

SEARCHING FOR HOME

FRIEDRICH SCHNACK

Friedrich Schnack was born in Rieneck, Germany in 1888. In addition to collections of poetry, he published several novels, children's books, and fairy tales, including the popular DER GLUCKSELIGE GARTNER. *His poems and fiction are lovingly based in his native region.*

When I pass into dust
I'll return in the evening wind,
I'll blow along the old lanes
where stars and legends gather.

I'll rattle at your door,
you'll know I'm out in the dark
and feel the deathly breath
when steps pass by.

A flame has consumed me,
from slumber and swelling grief,
I've sunk into the mother
from whom I blossomed.

I'll glide in long flashes
over your earthly hair.
I'll sit with you at the hearth
where my warmth once was.

I'll raise the candles in the room
and extinguish them as they crackle:
the moon will burn out in the tree,
the house crumble to ashes.

TRANSLATED BY NORBERT KRAPF FROM GERMAN

THE PRODIGAL SON

Roman Bar-or

Roman Bar-or was born in 1953 in a small Siberian village, where his father had been exiled by Stalin. In 1960, his family returned to Leningrad, now St. Petersburg, and he graduated from the university there in 1976. He emigrated to the United States in 1978. His book of poetry, **THE AGES ARRIVE AND GO**, *was published by Hermitage Books.*

Away: the ages arrive and go,
luscious leaves demand the snow.
Clouds lower on the horizon;
thoughts of white cross the sky.

And, as the snow-storm in a dream gathers,
so do the shadows of leaves flicker on the wind.
Slow pulsation; the fury of the wind.
The leaves scream, "I'm coming. I'm coming",
as they hold to their branches.

Always, the wind has had its channels
paved by leafage. The wind cradles the gaze
that has, excited, fled the eyes.
It's a motionless night when the snow flies
glimmering into the rivers, stacking on the hills
into the darkness — up to the sky!

Translated by Barry Wallenstein from Russian

AFTERWARDS

Harry Martinson

Born in Sweden in 1904, Harry Martinson wrote about nature as a sentient force. He was awarded The Nobel Peace Prize for Literature in 1974. He died in 1978.

After the battle of Helgoland

and after the battle of Utshima,

the sea dissolved the drifting logs of human carcasses,

treated them with its secret acids,

let albatrosses eat their eyes,

and with dissolving salts slowly restored them

to the prehistoric waters of the Cambrian Age,

for a fresh attempt.

Translated by W. H. Auden & Leif Sjoberg from Swedish

EIN LEBEN

Dan Pagis

Dan Pagis's biography appears with his poem "Winter's End".

The month she died

she is standing at her window,

a young woman with an elegant permanent

in a brown photograph,

pensively looking outside.

Outside, an afternoon cloud of 1934

is gazing at her — blurred, unfocused,

but faithful to her forever. Inside,

the someone looking at her is me,

almost four years old,

stopping my ball in air,

slowly stepping out of the photograph

and growing old, growing old

carefully, quietly

so as not to startle her.

Translated by Robert Friend & Shimon Sanbank from Hebrew

I ACCEPT

RADO

Rado's biography appears with his poem "I Am Black."

I accept that farewell

we bid the dead as necessary grief.

But bitter indeed are farewells

among the living who never meet.

TRANSLATED BY JEROME BROOKS & RAYMOND PATTERSON FROM MALAGASY

FROM THE AFTERWORLD

Sachiko Yoshihara

Sachiko Yoshihara is one of the most active women poets in Japan with several books of poetry to her credit. She won the Muroo Saisei Prize in 1965, and the Takami Jun Prize in 1974. She lives in Tokyo, where she was born.

> "Rewarding or punishing, the king
> of the afterworld is fearful."

This is my skull

lying from long ago in the grass.

Bamboo floats up skyward from the eyes.

But my left eye doesn't ache any more.

My flesh rotted and melted away.

As we turn into skulls our faces become the same—

no one can tell if it's me or you.

I faintly remember committing sins before birth,

bloody dark sins before my birth

> before that shiny edge of the basin for the newborn,
> that shiny edge for washing the newborn.

I die again, I live again, I make mistakes again.

Thank heaven, I forget those punishments for my sins.

It shouldn't happen, to see the future as clear as the past,

one measure of punishments for one measure of sin,

tenfold more for tenfold more sin...,
that should never happen.
I committed my sins with a trembling heart,
but they shouldn't be forgiven, either, for just one prayer.
In many burning evenings
I was ravished by floods of gentleness,
and if you say that's a sin
I bore many children of sin —
many shadows in the skull,
many dreams.

If you say it's a sin,
I will eat the filthy punishments
with my two lips painted red.
I will embrace the burning torture post.

Dogs nibble my bones
sweetly.

Bamboo sprouts float upward.
Everything swings in the wind.
From the dark hollow of my skull
these bamboo words float...
My left eye aches after all.

TRANSLATED BY YORIFUMI YAGUCHI & WILLIAM STAFFORD FROM JAPANESE

QUIETNESS   LIGHT   DARKNESS

LI-PO

Li-Po (701-762) was probably born in Central Asia, and spent his early years in Szechwan. For a short time, he served the Emperor Hsuan-tsung, and later, Prince Yung. Conditions and his temperament encouraged him to continue wandering. In more than 1,000 poems, he shows diversity, many moods, many seasons, many themes, much humor. He is still one of the most popular of great Chinese poets.

Quietness			Light	Darkness	
A	bright	dazed	I	I	my
very	reflection	amazed	lift	lower	previous
quiet	of	I	up	my	life
night	light	wonder	my	head	
thought			head		
	on	is			
	the	it	gaze	think	
	floor	frost	at	of	
	by	already?	the	my	
	my		Large	former	
	bed		Bright	home	
			Full		
			Moon		

TRANSLATED BY JOHN TAGLIABUE FROM MANDARIN

THE NIGHTINGALE

Marie de France

Marie de France, as her name indicates, was from the Ile de France, but she lived at the twelfth-century court of Henry II of England, where she earned her living as a poet. The **LAIS***, tales told in verse, are based on stories from Brittany.*

I will tell you of an adventure

From which the Bretons made a lai.

Methinks it was called Laustic;

if they called it that in their country

it is rossignol in French

and nightingale in English.

In St. Malo, in the vicinity

of a renowned town

there dwelt two chevaliers

and they had two large homes.

Because of the generosity of the two barons

the town had a good name.

One of the barons had a wife who was

wise, courteous and comely:

she held herself in high esteem

according to the custom and manner of the day.

The other was a bachelor
well-known among his equals
for prowess and for valor,
and he willingly paid honor:
he jousted often, distributing largesse,
and bestowing whatever he had.
He loved his neighbor's wife;
so much did he entreat her, so much did he beg her
and so much good was in him
that she loved him above all else,
partly for the good that she heard about him
and partly because he was nearby.
Discreetly and well they loved;
they were very secretive and kept watch
that they were not detected
nor disturbed, nor suspected.
And they were able to manage it very well
for they remained near their dwellings.
Their houses were quite close,
and their halls and keeps
were not separated by any barrier or dividing wall
except a high wall of dark-hued stone.
From the dame's chamber where she slept,
when she stood at the window,
she could talk to her friend,
and he, for his part, could talk to her,

and they exchanged their gifts
by throwing them, flinging them.
Nothing displeased them,
they were both much at ease,
except that they were unable to come
together at their pleasure,
for the woman was closely guarded
when her husband was in the country.
But to such an extent they had recourse,
that whether by night or by day
they were able to talk to each other;
no one could prevent them, much as he tried,
from coming to the window
and there amusing themselves.
Long they loved,
so much that one summer came,
when the copse and the meadow grew green again,
and the orchard was burgeoning.
Small birds nearby sang sweetly and joyfully,
balancing on flowertops.
He who knows love
should not be astonished at all this.
Of the chevalier, I will tell you the truth:
He heeded this with all his being,
and the dame on the other side of the wall,
both in sound and sight.

The nights when the moon shone
and her lord was asleep,
the dame often rose from beside him,
and attired herself in her mantel.
To the window she went,
for she knew that her lover
was suffering the same fate,
staying awake most of the night.
They took pleasure in looking at each other,
since they could have nothing more than that.

So long did she stand, so long did she get up
that her husband became angry with her,
and one time demanded
why she got up and where she went.
'Sire,' the lady answered him,
'he who has never heard the nightingale sing
has never known joy.
For that reason I stand here to look.
So sweetly I hear it at night
that it often seems to me a great delight;
the more it delights me and the more I see it,
I cannot shut my eye.'
When her husband heard what she said,
he laughed in a malicious way.
One thing he considered:

he would trap the nightingale.
He would not hear of a squire in his house
who did not make a snare or a fowler's net,
which afterwards they would put on the grass;
nor would he hear of a hazel tree or a chestnut tree
where they would not put a snare or bird-lime
until it was caught and held captive.
When the nightingale was taken to the lord
it was mortally wounded.
The seigneur held it in his hand and
to his wife's chamber he went.
'Lady,' said he, where are you?
Come here! Let's talk.
I have caught the nightingale
that has kept you awake so much.
From now on you will be able to lie in peace:
it will not wake you up anymore.'
When the lady had heard that,
she grew mournful and angry.
She demanded that he give it to her,
and he killed it in anger;
he broke its neck with his two hands —
and because he was acting in a villainous manner,
he cast the body on the lady,
staining her linen shift
just above her breast.

He went out of the chamber.
The lady took the little body,
crying bitterly and cursing
those who had caught the nightingale
and those who had made the snares and the fowler's nets,
for they had taken away a great pleasure from her.
'Alas,' said she, 'woe is me!
Nor will I now be able to rise at night
and go to the window to stand,
where I was wont to see my love.
One thing I know for sure:
he will think that I am faint-hearted;
of all this I must take counsel.
I will send him the nightingale,
it will tell the story.'
In a piece of samite,
interwoven with gold embroidery,
she had the tiny bird wrapped.
One of her squires was called,
and with her message was charged.
The squire came to the chevalier;
from his lady he gave greeting
all her message told him,
and gave him the nightingale.
When everything had been revealed and made known,
and he had listened well,

he was sad about how things had gone.
But he was not ill-mannered nor slow to act.
He had a small vessel made;
not of iron nor of steel;
but made of fine gold, studded with jewels
precious and dear.
A cover was well-fashioned.
He put the nightingale inside;
then he sealed up the relic,
and for the rest of his days carried it.

This story was told,
It could not long be concealed.
The Bretons made a *lai* of it:
Men call it 'The Nightingale.'

TRANSLATED BY MIRIAM BAKER FROM OLD FRENCH

RAZGLEDNICA

Miklos Radnoti

Miklos Radnoti, born in 1909, became one of Hungary's greatest lyric poets of his generation writing against Fascism. His first collection of poems appeared as early as 1924; several more followed. He studied French and Hungarian literature at the University of Szeged and received his doctorate in 1934. Because of his socialist leanings, he couldn't find a permanent teaching post and supported himself and his wife by translation and freelance articles. He was shot to death by German Nazis in Serbia having written his most mature and poignant poems while a prisoner. The notebook containing his last poems was found on his body when it was interred.

From Bulgaria rolls the thick, wild sound of cannons.

It pounces upon the mountain range, hesitates, and plummets.

Man, beast, carriage and thought collide;

the road rears up neighing; the maned sky gallops on.

In this frantic bedlam, you are constant within me;

you shine within my consciousness, forever still

and forever silent - an astonished angel beholding destruction,

or an insect burrowing into rotting bark.

(August 30, 1944 in the mountains)

Translated by Timea Szell from Hungarian

EPILOG

Manolis Anagnostakis

Manolis Anagnostakis is a leader of the Thessalonican school of poetry sometimes called "The Defeated", poets who came to maturity during the 1940s, and whose works reflect the most recent foreign occupation of Greece.

These could be the last lines ever

The last poets will write to the last readers

Because the poets of the future simply do not exist

The voices to come all died young

Their sad songs became birds

In some other sky lit by an alien sun

They became wild rivers and are running to the ocean

And you'll never separate out their waters

In their sad songs a lotus flowered

In its nectar we might even us we might grow younger.

Translated by Sam Abrams from Greek

Part II

Essays On the Art of Translating

INTRODUCTION: "TRADUTTORE, TRADITORE"

Elio Zappulla

"Traduttore, traditore", goes the old Italian adage. And it is an apt expression, for, as anyone who has tried it will tell you, attempting to translate poetry from one language into another almost always means a betrayal of the original. Everything gets translated, someone once said, except the poetry. What the reader frequently gets is "translatorese", which Ruth Rubin quotes John Ciardi as calling a "queer language-of-the-study that counts words but misses their living force." No matter how conscientious the translator, she or he must, however unwillingly, play the role of Judas, even though, as Claire Nicolas White so aptly puts it, "writers cannot afford to be unfaithful, for language is their only tool."

This is not to say that translations are useless or bad, or that they should not be attempted. Clearly, the choice lies between making an always frustrating attempt to convey at least the flavor of a poem to readers who do not know the original language, or else to leave such people in utter darkness. Martin Tucker reminds us that "translation is inevitably a choice of alternatives." Fundamentally, fidelity to the author's intent is usually the best that one can hope for in this difficult art: poetic devices, subtleties of sound, nuances of meaning are simply not transferable into another tongue. "It ends up pretty dead stuff," says Edward Field, who tells us of his own attempts to put Eskimo poetry into English.

The hope, of course, is that the translator is both competent and conscientious. When that happy combination occurs, and it sometimes does, we may just be lucky enough to be rewarded by versions that are works of art in their own right. Fitzgerald's remarkable **RUBAIYAT** is one example; Ciardi's splendid rendition of Dante is another; and of course Aaron Kramer's superb English versions of Yiddish and German poems belong preeminently to this felicitous category. Rather than translation as betrayal we have here instances of translations that are not only eminently faithful to the spirit and intent of the originals but also have obvious artistic merit of their own.

Attempting a translation is not unlike trying to tell someone how you felt as you stood on the rim of the Grand Canyon: you can search for whatever words will best convey what you experienced; you can show glossy prints of the Canyon, but you cannot fully recreate the experience, which your audience can only get by being there. You are therefore reduced to the status of a reporter. And so your competence and conscientiousness are vital if you are to convey at least a genuine sense of the "spirit" of the Grand Canyon. Those very same qualities are imperative for the intrepid translator if his readers are not to be misled and his author traduced.

Some of the knotty problems faced by translators are discussed in the essays that follow. Charles Mizzi recounts his struggles with rendering into English the nuances of a language like Maltese. The normal problems of translation are greatly magnified when languages so different from English are involved. When faced with the daunting task of translating, into any language, a writer like Umberto Eco, who peppers his dense Italian prose with phrases and sentences from a variety of other languages as well, the translator may feel confronted by the thirteenth labor of Hercules. Fritz G. Hensey discusses in some detail how William Weaver rendered Eco into English and Ricardo Pochtar transmuted him into Spanish. Hensey's observations and conclusions derive from an impressively detailed study of Eco's text. Ruth Rubin reminds us how much more complex the problem of verse translation can be when song texts are involved; here the translator must be sensitive to the nuances of music, to the intricacies of the art of singing.

Paul Forchheimer, whose polyglot background lends much weight to his arguments, insists that the translator needs to convey not only meaning, but the "peculiar style and flavor" of the original as well. Lief Sjoberg regales us with stories of how he and W.H. Auden got around the problems of converting the poetry of Ekelof into English verse. And in a close study of what is often really being translated from one language into another, as opposed to what ought to be translated, Richard E. Braun exhorts translators never to lose sight of the audience for whom the translation is intended: deep cultural differences between the original poet's audience and that of the translator must always be taken into account as one works at the task. Still, in Braun's words, "the meaning of the work is its final cause; the purpose of the translation should be that of the original."

PHOENICIA, MALTESE AND POETRY

CHARLES MIZZI

The last time I was asked for a translation was in the final exam for the required undergraduate foreign language course. With that B+, I thought I had bidden goodbye (and good riddance) to all required translations. Thinking a little further about the idea, however, I realized that all people are constantly doing translations of one kind or another. Spouses translate each other's grunts, h'mms, and even silences into some message of assent, wonder or tacit agreement. Posture, tones of voice, even movements of an eyebrow, translate and even modify whole messages.

Very little further thought made me realize that I have made even "technical" translations from one foreign tongue to another, several times to my wife and family. A few of these are interesting and illuminating of the vagaries and similarities of language codes. My native tongue is Maltese, a Semitic language sharing roots with Arabic, classical Coptic and ancient Hebrew. It is thought to most closely resemble the Aramaic of Biblical times. Of the many "native" expressions I have used that have been adopted by my family, two are illustrative of how languages as widely separated as Maltese and English can have basic common concepts.

"Ghandu l-geddum" is an expression literally translated as "he has a pronounced (long) chin." In English, "he has a long face." "Iddejjaqni" (unpronounceable in English) literally translates to "(it) makes me narrow" or in English, "I feel bothered, irritated." These seem a pretty clear indication of how the human body may be a basic language medium, at least for feelings. Concepts and literature, particularly the uses of literature, however, can be a totally different story.

I have often wondered, for example, how the Maltese words for writing and lying evolved. Both sound almost exactly alike with only the softness of the second consonant making this crucial distinction between <u>nikteb</u> (to write) <u>nigdeb</u> (to prevaricate).

The Maltese people are descendants of the Phoenicians, who spread (but did not invent) the antecedent of the alphabet currently in use. In spite of this, Maltese was not commonly written until the middle of the 19th century. Such 'literary' works that were written - political, religious or cultural - were written in Latin, and later in Italian. Some of these are thought to go back to the Punic Wars in which Malta, originally a colony of Carthage, was involved. Folk tales of course existed, as they did in all societies, but in Malta these were transmitted orally. Poetry existed, too, but this was generally aimed at extolling someone's virtue or attacking his faults. As such, being mostly topical and contemporary, these poems were evanescent. Another form, now being revived at "folkloric" events came into play which was more of a contest. In this event, usually at some celebration or social occasion, two "antagonists" would be chosen. Each would be required to declaim in rhyme either how good, strong, virtuous, or handsome they, their families, friends or womenfolk, horses, or hunting dogs are; or how awful are the other side's. Each antagonist would take turns, verse for verse, singing at the top of their voices, well-lubricated by the local wine, simultaneously cheered and booed by both sides until the winner was declared. This winner was not the cleverer or wittier or more imaginative, but the more long-winded. Of course, none of this was ever taken seriously (and therefore recorded), else blood feuds would have decimated the population.

As in most cultures, nursery rhymes and jingles recited while rocking baby to sleep, or during jump-rope and skipping-games were common. Some of these were total nonsense, but made pleasant rhyming sounds.

One that I remember goes like this:

>Am pam pam pilili pililenza
>Koo ja fa kutuli kutuletto.
>Ala ala mi
>tu sevnti
>am pam pam
>pililim pim pom.

This makes absolutely no sense in any language I have ever tried.

Many Mediterranean cultures also impart folkways, mores or moral or religious lessons through nursery rhymes. Two that have persisted in my family are an example of each of these. The first is clearly a biblical lesson. In Maltese it goes like this:

> Sant'Anna u San Giakkin,
> Il-Madonna u 'l-Bambin
> Xorti kella dik Sant'Anna
> Il-Bambin aedila "Nanna".

The English translation of this rhyme is:

> Saint Ann and Saint Jacob
> Our Young Christ and his ma;
> Oh how lucky was Saint Ann
> Our Lord called her "Grandma"!

The second refers to some custom, possibly part of a courting ritual:

> Katarin, gibtlek lampuka,
> Katarin kebbes in-nar,
> Katarin iftah it-tiqa,
> Lahhi johrog id-duhhan.

The verse translates into English like this:

> Katarin, I brought you a fish.
> Katarin, fire up the grill.
> Katarin, open up the window
> or smoke this room will fill.

A vast bulk of traditional poetry was epigrammatic, dedicated to nice, important figures. An example of this is:

> TO A POET (buried here)
> Oh poet buried in this grave
> Who gave your life to poetry and verse
> Your bones, a pile of dust, won't fill a thimble,
> But the beauty your eyes saw, fills the universe.
> (from **THE MALTESE MUSE, AN ANTHOLOGY OF MALTESE POETS**)

Longer poems, of course, exist. Some are of epic proportions. However, attempts at their translation, besides taxing this writer and his relatives, would probably only confuse a reader not familiar with the fine distinctions of Middle Eastern and Mediterranean history and ethnography. Translating from Maltese presents the unique difficulty of bringing a language that was old and fixed before the rise of the Hellenic world, with the accretions of more than thirty centuries, into the flexibility and richness of modern English.

It is this writer's hope that these modest attempts will help to illustrate the poet's art of translating everyday life into everlasting verities.

TRANSLATING THE ESKIMOS

Edward Field

In the mid-sixties, I was asked to "do" (I purposefully choose an ambiguous word) a book of Eskimo poetry as part of an experimental teaching program for fifth grade students. In choosing me, the determining factor for the committee was that I was the only poet they could find whose poetry was understandable to ten year-olds. This does not dismay me, since I have never been very "bright" about poetry, and write for people like myself.

As source material, I was given **THE RASMUSSEN ARCHIVES**, the record of the Danish explorer's expeditions to the Arctic between 1902 and 1933, four thick volumes, luckily with interlinear translations of the Eskimo material. The poems I made out of selections of this material were later published by Delacorte as a children's book, **ESKIMO SONGS AND STORIES**. But the introduction I wrote for it never appeared, having been jettisoned by the editor as unsuitable. Slightly revised, and with samples of the poems added, here it is. (I must add that the poems were censored for children, on the dubious grounds, I suppose, that children must never see the basic functions referred to in print. For example, "Grandma went behind the house to pee" became "Grandma went behind the house", and four of the more scatological and sexual poems had to wait for print until my book **VARIETY PHOTOPLAYS**).

These poems are based on conversations Rasmussen had with the Eskimos of the Netsilik tribe who live north of Hudson Bay. Rasmussen, part Eskimo himself, had grown up in Greenland with Eskimo relatives and friends, so their language was his second tongue after Danish. Throughout his life, he made a number of expeditions to the people of the Arctic, becoming a one-man bridge between the Eskimos and us, demonstrating how communication can be established with another race, so that we learn from them, not just enslave and exploit and destroy them, as it is in the Western tradition to do to native peoples. Rasmussen wrote down their legends, history, life experiences, jokes and tales, descriptions of how they did things like hunting caribou and seal, songs they made up for fun or magic or out of sorrow, and how they felt about life and death and the universe — in short, almost every aspect of Eskimo life.

> In the very earliest time,
> when both people and animals lived on earth,
> a person could become an animal if he wanted to
> and an animal could become a human being....
> All spoke the same language.
> (from "Magic Words")

He took all this down exactly as the Eskimos told it to him, and this makes a problem — for spoken words are significantly different from written. When someone talks, you hear the feelings expressed by the tone of voice and vocal emphasis, and physical gestures and facial expressions comment on and act out the meaning, so the words themselves tell only part of the story. Words you write have to be more complete and include the very sound of the voice. If you just write down spoken words, they very often don't make too much sense and get across. The feelings are lost, as well as the jokes, both of which are important in communication. And then in translating from one language to another you lose more. It ends up pretty dead stuff, so I felt my job was to bring it to life again.

> BIG POPPA OWL: Our two sons ought to be back soon from hunting. Keep a look out, Momma....
> BIG MOMMA OWL: There they come, our darlings, each dragging a marmot!
> BIG POPPA OWL: Yum, yum, I can't wait.
> (from "A Peek Into An Owl's House, Or, Just Like Humans")

These "Eskimo" poems of mine, from Rasmussen's material, attempt a portrait of the Eskimo, without going into the complicated subject of meeting up with the white man and how our technology and morals affected the daily life of Eskimos and their ancient ways. I also selected material that I felt was appropriate for poems — of course, there is no limit on what can be in a poem, even a recipe for keeping young-looking (as in one of the Eskimo poems not in this book because of its discussion of the therapeutic use of dog turds, making it, in the view of adults, unsuitable for a children's book):

> When I was just a girl
> I once took a beauty treatment
> recommended by our medicine man:
> Grandma took me out
> and found old dried-up dog turds for me.
> I had to put each turd on my tongue
> keeping it in my mouth until it was soft,
> then rub myself with it
> all over my breasts and stomach.
> That is where I got my lovely figure and vitality from.
>
> (from "Beauty Cure")

In reading these poems I wanted you to be able to sense a real person speaking, in this case, an Eskimo person (or rather, Inuit, for the name Eskimo is a French invention), with all his history and his humanity. There are no people more delightful, though to tell the truth I only know them through authors like Rasmussen. So, what I found myself doing, was to recreate a people like my own, the Jews. As a result these poems came out half Jewish, half Eskimo. This is not so ridiculous as it sounds, for I could sense that the Eskimos had much in common with the Jews: their sense of humor (for Jews also consider the joke a major form of human wisdom, if not divine truth); feelings like sympathy and tenderness (banned from modern poetry as sentimentality), that Jews consider more important than being tough; the earthiness, as in much Jewish humor, making some of these poems sound a little coarse to us; and a general warmth and schmaltziness that is equally Jewish and Eskimo — all qualities that I feel are anti-Puritan and a corrective to the limitations of our Anglo-Saxon traditions.

> When the meat cache was frozen solid that winter
> and we could not break it open,
> we called on The Great Farter to help us.
> (from "The Great Farter")

Our literature is so indoctrinated with the English tradition (even the language transmits it) that reading the words of different peoples is a healthy thing, especially those of non-Christian peoples, who have not inherited our deep guilts and our foolish restrictions on sex and feelings. In other words the Inuit cry when unhappy, laugh when happy, maybe kill when angry, and say what they think and feel.

> The Owl hollered back, "You dirty bird,
> so you won't have me for a husband?
> Then I hope you end up a tidbit between
> someone's teeth!
> (from "Courting Song")

The Jews and the Eskimos also share a traditional device in story-telling — laughter-through-tears. This means that you get your listeners laughing and then make them cry, or get them crying and make them laugh, so they don't know what they are doing and come out of the experience opened up, even illuminated, about human nature, which of course is both funny and tragic, and who can separate them?

> Grandma turned a little odd in spring:
> She took a caterpillar in and mothered it.
> She put it down her sleeve
> while she went about her housework,
> letting it suck like a baby on her skin,
> and soon it grew so big and fat and happy
> it said, Jeetsee-jeetsee.
> (from "Grandma Takes A Foster Child")

There is no need to remind anyone what the Jews have

suffered. The Eskimos, added to what the white man has put them through, suffer a different and unrelenting kind of hardship, and during a time of famine the aged must voluntarily go to their deaths for the sake of saving others, not heroically but just go off in the snow and die, so there is one less mouth to feed.

> How would anyone who has eaten his fill
> be able to understand the madness of hunger?
> We only know that we all want so much to live!
> (from "Hunger")

I put into these poems my own background, my own nature, my voice (especially my mother's voice telling me tales of her shtetl in Poland) without much distortion, I believe, of what Eskimos are really like.

So these poems are not poetry by the Eskimos (the poems are by me) but they are poetry of the Eskimos, fashioned out of their special words.

LANGUAGE AS HOMELAND
or Finding the American Voice

Claire Nicolas White

Ever since my own memoir was published, I have become aware of others recently that are similar, that may, in fact, indicate a trend of our time: the memoir that bridges two cultures, that tries to span a lost childhood with an American present. The books I shall refer to in particular are by women established here in the United States, yet with different roots.

I was first struck by Eva Hoffman's **LOST IN TRANSLATION**. Its brilliant title is the metaphor for the theme of uprootedness, the shedding of one culture to adopt another. This also involves a switch in language, not the least difficulty for a writer to face.

"Ma langue, c'est ma patrie," said a clever Frenchman whose name I have forgotten. It may well have been my own uncle, the poet-playwright George Neveux, who knew what he was talking about. His mother was a White Russian, and as a child he was brought up in that language. His tale, in fact, was bizarre, for he was the illegitimate son of a French officer, and he claims to have been hidden in a cellar, a true no-man's land, until his mother's legal husband died. "The cellar window looked out on a street, and all I could see were the legs of people going by. I judged mankind by its feet," he quipped. His imagination was so vivid, having come from this Russian hiding place to Belgium where he was boarded with a local peasant woman, finally to Paris, that I never quite trusted the truth of his tales. His having had to leap over two hurdles, illegitimacy, then exile, made me realize that the more distant the origin of the writer, the more open to invention.

If language then is a writer's homeland, it is also a writer's companion for better or worse. Writers cannot afford to be unfaithful, for language is their only tool. Without it they are mute. It is of course possible to be multilingual, but only superficially. A final choice has to be made. Like the courtesan with several lovers, such a relationship remains frivolous. "When I fall in love, I am seduced by language," says Eva Hoffman. It is possible to flirt in several languages, but to express true love one must be possessed heart and soul, in waking and dreaming, in speaking and reading, in rhyme and in prose, in song and in chatter, by one dominant language. Again, in Eva's words, "The thought that there are parts of the language I'm missing can induce a small panic in me, as if the totality of the world and the mind were coeval with the totality of language."

Eva Hoffman left Poland at the age of thirteen to settle first in Canada, in the 50's, with her family. She soon found that certain expressions, as well as feelings and nuances, are untranslatable. She was thrown right away into Canadian-American schools, among American schoolmates whose parents had "made good", while her own struggled to support their family with a second-hand furniture business.

I myself was fourteen when I came from the Netherlands, in 1940, to New York, where I did my high school studies at the French Lycee. For me, French was a transition, the language of adolescence, which I fell in love with (not only literally speaking), and which wiped out my Dutch, the language of childhood. From then on, we spoke French at home to please my mother who was Belgian, and to continue the mode of thought of my studies. It retarded my americanization which was, therefore, more gradual than Eva's. French was still European, the society of French-speaking emigres, all more or less impoverished, like our own. Not till I went to college did I begin to actually think in English and to discover it as literature. It became, for me, the language of adulthood. I majored in English, for it seemed to be remarkably hospitable, flexible. My teachers did not consider my other languages an impediment, but an advantage, and I felt an intense need to translate for my new companions my "otherness", my way of thinking, my language.

Another memoir published somewhat earlier by the granddaughter of the Russian writer Andreiev, is **ISLAND IN TIME**, by Olga Carlisle. It covers the period of the war years, 1940-45, that she spent with her extended family of Russian emigres on the island of Oleron, on the Atlantic coast of France. Though her parents and aunts felt intensely Russian, exiled because of politics from a country Olga never knew, the island became an idyllic miniature world in itself for her. It was, moreover, a temporary one. It was understood that they would leave when the war ended to move to the United States. It was rather like my transitory world at the French Lycee. "Since my early childhood I had been explaining myself to strangers," she writes. "An oddity, a girl without a country." It was not till later when she went to Russia that she felt she was "one of them". Her father still had felt that "real life" was somewhere else, in distant Russia. At the end of her book she concludes, "As a young woman I lived among American writers. They resembled the Russians of my early years. They, too, were searching for their lost country, their childhood." Perhaps she found in the intense mobility of Americans who rarely live in the place where they were born a similar feeling of "You can't go home again".

Is this, then, what all writers of memoirs are looking for, a lost childhood? The more distant, the more impossible to revisit, the more vivid it seems to become, because it is really an imaginary recreation. "I remember Cracow literally from my dreams," says Eva.

This also seems evident from the extraordinary books by the Chinese Americans Maxine Hong Kingston and Amy Tan. Though not necessarily in the form of memoirs, they nevertheless explore a past beyond childhood through the tales of their mother, so that this prenatal homeland of theirs is recreated entirely in the imagination. It acquires a mythical "otherness", which is exotic, but also intrusive on the American lives of the authors. In **THE JOY LUCK CLUB**, Amy Tan has one of her young women say, "As soon as my feet touched China, I became Chinese."

"It is painful to be consciously of two worlds," Anne Roiphe quotes a Polish immigrant in her book, **A GENERATION WITHOUT MEMORY**. But to willfully forget one's ancestry is a tremendous tour de force, an amputation that can victimize a person. Ann Roiphe describes her immigrant father as being, "An American, that's all...He became so American that he was like a pioneer, a trapper in a distant forest of his making." While teaching writing workshops in nursing homes to older immigrants who barely spoke English, I myself met the same fierce loyalty to the adopted country over and over again. "We're American, that's that," they'll say. But this denial of the past, this "assimilation by definition means some self-hate," says Roiphe. The more humble the background of the immigrant, the more he seems to think that he is improving his lot by ignoring his past, by forgetting his native language, even if this means being limited to broken English.

Both Eva Hoffman and Ann Roiphe seem to have read **THE EDUCATION OF HENRY ADAMS** with a measure of envy, since this memoir is so confidently patrician, so almost smugly American.

Eva writes, "My American friends' explorations are a road to a new instead of an ancestral wisdom," but at the same time, "all immigrants and exiles know the peculiar restlessness of an imagination that can never again have faith in its own absolutism. Only exiles are truly irreligious." If she is then aware, on the one hand, of the untrammeled freedom of contemporary American thought, she also regrets the loss of a tradition a Henry Adams could still afford.

It seems to me evident that in order to heal the split between the two lives, the two languages, the first part, the "shed" childhood has to be retold in the adopted tongue so as to become part of the whole. To entirely belong to the new country, that part of life which preceded it must be translated, integrated, to bridge a schizophrenic existence. Language then provides one consistently unifying element. When writing my book I found that this retelling also explained to me who this other self that spoke in different tongues was. Now, when I return to Holland, the landscape, the food, the customs are so familiar that I feel disconcertingly at home there. Only the language is no longer quite my own. I speak it as if I were an actress playing a part, and catch myself being quite different from the persona I have become, the one who has found a home in the American idiom. In France, too, I communicate with total ease. I could slip into a French mode of thinking, of gesturing, into a system of jokes, of inflections learned during adolescence. But again, it would be a loss of the identity I acquired with such effort during all these year, an essential unfaithfulness.

Interestingly enough, the editor who worked on the book with me noticed that in the latter chapters the language spoken during the American part of my life had not been subjected to a subconscious process of translation. It may also be that to distance myself from this former existence I exaggerate the foreignness of my childhood. It is the difference that is emphasized, the contrast between that country and this one that I dwell on. If it is a plea for understanding from my American readers, it is also an explaining of my former self to my new self, in the language that now possesses me.

So these memoirs are less a factual record than a recreation in a new language. The more distant we are from it in place, as well as time, the more we invent it, the more magical it becomes. It is precisely these attempts to translate the untranslatable that makes the memoir a challenge for our time.

TRANSLATING WITH W. H. AUDEN

Leif Sjoberg

"Why? Do you have a contract?" replied W. H. Auden the first time I earnestly posed the question: would he consider translating Ekelof's poetry into English? I had to pause, slightly embarrassed because I had no contract, and Auden offered a bit of advice: "One should never translate on spec. It's bad for everybody's morale!" I politely suggested that not much poetry would have been translated into English had it not been for initiatives of poetry lovers labouring on speculation. The (legitimate or illegitimate) concern for profit among major British and American publishers creates a kind of "gold curtain" that tends to insulate English readers from the rest of the world's poetry.

To illustrate how difficult it was to get poetry from "neglected" (minor) languages published in English, I mentioned that in the early 1960's Ekelof's poetry had been translated "on spec" by no less a poet than Muriel Rukeyser - in collaboration with me - and that a publisher (after several months) returned the book-length manuscript - unopened! The accompanying rejection letter, composed of select phrases from a variety of form letters, amounted to both a "yes" and a "no". How could this happen? Later, when pressed for an explanation, the editor excused himself by saying, "Sending Swedish poetry to us (i.e., a reputable university press), in whatever translation, is like sending us Outer Mongolian poetry: it does not stand much of a chance, because we have no market for it."

This story may have made a certain impact on Auden. He gradually became convinced that the competition to get good foreign poetry published in English was fierce, perhaps unfair, and might even, under unfortunate circumstances, act like a form of censorship against his colleague poets in "critical" languages. But what could he do to alleviate the situation? Even if he were to care enough about certain poetry to donate his time and translate it, what difference would it make? The basic problems would remain the same.

In this, of course, Auden was right. His reluctance to get involved was, I suspect, due to his great workload, his wish not to appear one-sided in his interest in things Swedish, and his realization of the many problems to be faced. What I intend to discuss in this essay is merely a few of these problems, primarily with reference to unidentified quotations, with or without quotation marks - i.e., "borrowed" lines - and what they do, or fail to do, for a translation.

The collaboration between Auden and myself did not begin with Ekelof. I was teaching Swedish and Scandinavian literature at Columbia University when I first submitted samples of literal translations, as well as copies of Ekelof's originals in Swedish, to Mr. Auden. Nothing was heard from his quarter for several months, so I began to expect I would never hear from him, but in the autumn of 1963 he called me and asked if I had read Dag Hammarskjold's secret diary, **VAGMARKEN**; he wondered whether I would like to work with him on an English translation of that book. Naturally, I was delighted. We met in his apartment on the Lower East Side, usually for tea. He was always very pleasant to work with and strict about keeping appointments.

It turned out that Dag Hammarskjold was quite sympathetic to Ekelof's poetry, and even quoted three lines in **VAGMARKEN** as the fifth item under the head "1953":

> Kommer den, kommer den ej,
> dagen da gladjen blir stor,
> dagen da sorgen blir liten?
>
> (Will it come, or will it not,
> The day when the joy becomes great,
> The day when the grief becomes small?[1])

In **MARKINGS** Auden added underneath this unidentified quotation: "(Gunnar Ekelof)". These were the first lines of Ekelof's poetry that Auden rendered into English - but not the last. He also found time to translate several poems or prose poems by Werner Aspenstrom (b. 1918), Johannes Edfelt (b. 1904), Erik Lindegren (1920-68), Artur Lundkvist (b. 1906), Harry Martinson (1904-78), and Karl Vennberg (b. 1910). There was also one major translation, consisting of 51 out of the 62 poems of Par Lagerkvist's book **AFTONLAND**, which

Auden had completed but not revised, and which appeared in a bilingual edition as **EVENING LAND/AFTONLAND**.[2] **EVENING LAND** was, in fact, Lagerkvist's ninth collection of poetry, and it remains the first and only book of his poetry in English. It is to Auden's everlasting credit that he performed this service, which no other poet had found possible to do. At one time, though, when faced with a particularly "gloomy" poem by Lagerkvist, Auden confessed in a note, perhaps tongue in cheek: "My decorous Anglican piety is rather shocked."

Whatever Dag Hammarskjold may or may not have had in common with the modernists in poetry, the English poet had a high opinion of him, as expressed in the **ENCOUNTER** article[3] and in the foreword of **MARKINGS**.[4] Auden never found any entirely new image in **MARKINGS**, but an abundance of intriguing and personal statements. The technique Hammarskjold sometimes employed in quoting without quotation marks or accompanying (explanatory) notes posed no problems for Auden who (with my assistance) located the many biblical references in **VAGMARKEN**. I think he liked the idea that he was the first to do so. (The Swedish edition had identified neither Hammarskjold's quotations nor any of the allusions or references. As far as I know, such notes appeared in the Swedish, German, and other versions only *after* Auden's groundwork had been published - and with no credit given to Auden.)[5] In the limited time available for the translation and research, the difficulties were such that, in instances, even Auden's enormous reading proved inadequate to solve the problems. This was one reason why Auden (for the first time, I believe) went to Sweden in the spring of 1964. With the eager assistance of diplomat friends of Dag Hammarskjold's, but above all of the poet Erik Lindegren, most of the still unresolved attributions, including references to Thomas Browne's **RELIGIO MEDICI** (29 July-16 August 1956, in **MARKINGS**),[6] were taken care of.

When Hammarskjold in a "marking" dated 25 November 1956 quoted in Norwegian;

> Hvis alt Du gaf foruden Lifvet,
> saa ved at Du har intet gifvet.

>   (If you give all, but life retain
>   Your gift is nothing and in vain.[7])

Auden simply added: "(Ibsen: Brand)" and, since he was even able to keep the rhyme, it caused him no problem as a translator. In a "marking" dated 13 February-13 March 1961, Hammarskjold wrote:

> O Du som forde oss till detta sjalens nakna liv, ode
> som svavar over vattnen, skall Du en jordisk kvall beratta
> vems handen ar som ifor oss en sagas brinnande tunika[8]

Quotation marks and source were left out. The word *tunika*, tunic, almost ruled out a Swedish author - indeed, the author was St. John Perse.

In "Letter to Lord Byron" Auden had written (August 1936),[9] "at any language other than my own, I'm no great shakes...". But since that time his German, at least, had advanced considerably, and as a result German was sometimes used for expressions and sentences in my literal translation of **VAGMARKEN**, when English equivalents were unavailable or stilted. Although Auden never studied Swedish and therefore needed linguistic expertise, he had a remarkable grasp of what Swedish texts were all about - presumably largely due to his knowledge of German, but also due to his being a genius with words. This was apparent when it was necessary to locate specific words - he frequently knew at least the general area in which to search for a word. Sometimes he found the particular word or sentence, even before I could point it out to him.

One of Auden's strong points was his logic. He could rearrange the order of clauses when logic demanded that one clause precede the other, or when the meaning would be clearer that way in English. Since English is so much richer in vocabulary than Swedish, he now and then found fault with the original. Having considered the most obvious alternatives for a word and, repeatedly, being reminded of the literal translation, he might still say, "logic demands that *this* word be used", rattling off a number of arguments. Usually those were hard to refute, if not irrefutable. When I persisted and said, "Let us see what the text says!" and read straight from the original in front of us, playing over again the literal translation with possible variations, he might shake his big head and say "No, my dear, that won't do! It can't be said like that in English!" or "That's not English!"

The many long, compound words in Swedish and the multiple genitives ending in "s" naturally caused some trouble, but Auden never despaired while working at the translation. He always started "full steam ahead" and with great enthusiasm. What was gained in vividness and geniality through this method was partially offset by occasional infelicitous interpretations, due primarily to lack of time for research. One such example for which I was responsible comes to mind. In one of the "markings" from 1952, Hammarskjold writes:

>Give me something to die for-!
>
>Die Mauern stehen
>sprachlos und kalt, die Fahnen
>klirren im Winde.
>
>What makes loneliness an anguish
>Is not that I have no one to share my burden,
>But this:
>I have only my own burden to bear.[10]

Hammarskjold had naturally not identified the German quotations from Holderlin, which Auden translated as follows:

>The walls stand
>speechless and cold, the banners
>faffle in the wind.

The trouble was that "klirren" (rattle) seemed to us an odd verb to apply to "Fahnen" (flag, banner); in the translation Auden used "faffle". What we failed to realize was that "Fahnen", flag in German, had developed from Old High German *fano*, akin to Old English *fana*, banner; this in turn was related to *vane*, weather vane. The correct literal translation would therefore have been "vanes rattle," rather than "banners faffle".

Occasionally, Auden would exclude a word or two if they were repetitious or superfluous; he found a contracted sentence more effective. This happened in the translation of Ekelof's **SELECTED POEMS** where, in one poem, four to five lines were condensed into one, which Ekelof authorized, with some consternation. On occasion Auden would say: "I think we had better abandon that one; it's getting to be too complicated, and too far from the original." (This applied only to the rhymed poems by Lagerkvist, published as **EVENING LAND/AFTONLAND**.)

I made sure that on his visit to Stockholm (via Iceland) Auden would meet Ekelof, who lived at Sigtuna, a town on the Lake Malar, 45 minutes from the capital. Both Georg Svensson, of Bonniers (Auden's Swedish publisher), and Lindegren had previous commitments and could not go to Sigtuna, but the poet Osten Sjostrand (b. 1925) who had translated the Auden-Kallman libretto of Stravinsky's **THE RAKE'S PROGRESS**[11] accompanied Auden to the Ekelof home.[12] Ekelof, "a modern mystic",[13] as his friend Lindegren called him, was decidedly non-Christian, non-dogmatic, and an introvert, "an outsider", while, of course, Auden was a believer, an extrovert and an insider; nonetheless they could be expected to have lots of things to discuss: both were deeply appreciative of music and modern poetry, after all. In leafing through my copy of Ekelof's **L'ALFRANDSKAPER (ELECTIVE AFFINITIES)**[14] in New York, Auden had found Ekelof's translations of Petronius, Villon, Baudelaire, Rimbaud, Whitman, Butler, Joyce, Leon-Paul Fargue, D. H. Lawrence (which seemed to surprise Auden), Jalalu'd-din-Rumi, the Sufi mystic who was so central to the Swedish poet - but also a substantial presentation of Apollinaire and another of Ekelof's favorites, Desnos. Among the "elective affinities" Auden was himself represented by a Swedish version of "Musee des Beaux Arts" (which Auden promptly asked me to translate - or some lines of it - back into English, *prima vista*, while he waited, so to speak, and since Ekelof's translation was felicitous and my knowledge of the original was reasonably good, I think Ekelof came out rather well.) Auden mentioned that he had been spending Christmas in Brussels when he wrote the poem. It seemed like such an excellent idea to get these two together.

Auden, perhaps comparing his own shabby apartment on New York's St. Mark's Place, thought Ekelof's house, "rather extravagant" for a poet - the furniture being "expensive looking" antiques. (Most of them, actually, were inherited, but he admitted that the setting was idyllic.) He found Ekelof "severely depressed", perhaps "due to a drinking problem". On the other hand, Ekelof found Auden "diplomatic but cordial".[15] A few days later Ekelof commented on how "amiable" (*angenamt*: very pleasant) and how "nicely shrivelled" (*trevligt skrumpen*) Auden had appeared - and how 'ignorant of languages'.[16] This, no doubt, referred to Auden's disinclination towards the French language, which surprised some of the people he met in Stockholm, and his limited familiarity with Italian, Latin, and Greek, and perhaps also Near Eastern languages. (Ekelof had studied Hindustani for a few months at the London School of Oriental Studies in 1926 and had taken one semester of Persian at Uppsala University, 1926-7. In 1958, the same year that he became a member of the Swedish Academy, he was given a Ph.D *honoris causa* at Uppsala.) The tea-drinking was, apparently, pleasant enough - but, as Ekelof put it, there was "noll contact"[17] (*sic!*), zero contact.

The caution with which these very considerable poets approached each other precluded real friendship beyond superficial cordiality. It was only much later than Auden took such an interest in Ekelof that he asked me for "some stuff" to translate. He got Ekelof first. It proved to be to Auden's liking. The cooperation from Gunnar Ekelof was remarkable, for Ekelof was then fatally ill - his wife, Ingrid Ekelof, read and commented on the translations as they progressed. Auden was very pleased with the results: "We've got the best", he said, broadly smiling.

Ekelof had thirteen collections of poetry to his credit - including **SENT PA JORDEN (LATE ON EARTH**, 1932); **FARJESANG (FERRY SONG**, 1941); **NON SERVIAM** (1945); **STROUNTES (TRIFLINGS**, 1955); **OPUS INCERTUM** (1959); and **EN MOLNA-ELEGI (A MOLNA ELEGY**, 1960), "a major translation by a major poet", according to Goran Printz-Phalson, and published here for the first time in English; as well as an assortment of selected poems (1949, 1956, and 1965) plus volumes of his essays and translations from many languages but above all from the French - when in 1965 he commenced what was to be perhaps his most remarkable achievement: a trilogy, consisting of **DIWAN OVER FURSTEN AV EMIGION (DIWAN OVER THE PRINCE OF EMGION**, 1965), **SAGAN OM FATUMEH (THE TALE OF FATUMEH**, 1966) and **VAGVISARE TILL UNDERJORDEN (GUIDE TO THE UNDERWORLD**, 1967).

Almost all of the poems of **DIWAN** and **FATUMEH** were translated by Auden and authorized by Ekelof, with the exception of those few poems that did not work in English, and those that Auden considered redundant or repetitive. Occasionally Auden was so pleased with a poem that he read it aloud for comments, although I was his entire audience. One of those poems was "Ayiasma":

> In the calm water I saw mirrored
> Myself, my soul:
> Many wrinkles
> The beginnings of a turkey-cock neck
> Two sad eyes
> Insatiable curiosity
> Incorrigible pride
> Unrepentant humility
> A harsh voice
> A belly slit open
> And sewn up again
> A face scarred by torturers
> A maimed foot
> A palate for fish and wine
> One who longs to die
> Who has lain with some
> In casual beds - but for few
> Has felt love - a for him
> Necessary love
> One who longs to die
> With someone's hand in his
> Thus I see myself in the water
> With my soiled linen left behind me when I am
> > gone
> A Kurdic Prince called a dog

> By both Rumaians and Seldjuks
> In the water my bald forehead:
> All the mangled tongues
> Which have convinced me
> That I am mute
> And those stains on my shirt
> Which water will never wash out -
> Indelible like blood, like poison
> The stains of the heretic
> Shall strike them like the plague
> With still blacker stains.[19]

The note appended to the poem reads: "Ayiasma (Hagiasma): purifying well. The water cult is alive in Greece and the Near East. A glass of cold water is the holy welcoming drink among the people." Another "ayiasma", beginning,

> The black image
> Framed in silver worn to shreds by kisses[17]

Auden cared for particularly. He also read the last poem of **FATUMEH** with admiration:

> Moon! Moon! so might a poor farmer's wife see you
> When, having driven one furrow with her wooden
>   plough
> She raises her face
> And wipes the sweat from her forehead
> Before starting upon the next one
>
> -Are you an egg in space
> A hen's egg with a wrinkled shell
> Or are you a wind egg that dimly mirrors
> Our fields and mountains?
>
> But the angel grips her arm
> and points to where
> A Star has just fallen

Leaving an empty space
Inside the Moon's sickle.[20]

In this poem elements form music and art fused into a unity of their own. The original poem begins with "Avgo! Avgo!", and has here been translated "Moon! Moon!" (if I remember correctly, at the suggestion of Nikos Stangos, the British poet and translator). Ekelof was a great fan of Boris Christoff's interpretations of Moussorgsky's song cycles, and played some of his recordings over and over again. On the day when I had an appointment with Ekelof at his home at Sigtuna, he was tired and tense. Almost the only subject he could converse on with any flair at all was music, and whichever way the conversation turned, it always seemed to come back to Moussorgsky; when the topic was exhausted, the conversation started over again with the marvelous bass, Boris Christoff (I believe Ekelof had seen Chaliapin in Paris in the 'Thirties). The session ended with Ekelof playing LP records of children's songs by Moussorgsky. He hummed and gesticulated, he lay back on his bed, his face became peaceful, and he fell asleep, while the music of Moussorgsky continued. One of his favorites was a lullaby with a recurring phrase, "Baju! Baju!", (Lull! Lull!), which Ekelof, according to Ingrid Ekelof, heard as "Avgo! Avgo!", thus associating it with the Greek word for "egg". In his imagination Ekelof identified this song "Avgo! Avgo!" with a reproduction of a fresco from a Serbian church, in which an angel standing before an old shepherd points up towards the sky, his arm around the shepherd's shoulders. The old man looks up with pious awe. In the picture there is neither egg nor moon! But the poet made the Russian "Baju!" into the Greek "Avgo!", then made his egg into a moon: moved by the shepherd's simple piety, and his own profound experience before the sublimity of the scene, Ekelof sang "Avgo! Avgo!". Later he went on to make the old shepherd into an old woman, thereby further underscoring the female dominance - the almost frenzied devotion to women - in **THE TALE OF FATUMEH**. Auden was pleased and amused by these transformations.

About his **DIWAN** poems Ekelof wrote to me, in English, in the spring of 1965 this revealing, previously unpublished note. It should be remembered that he was in a hospital at the time and had no access to a copy editor, even if he had wanted one:

In four weeks, beginning in Constantinople, I have
written a mystical ode of some fifty or sixty poems,
translated from the idiom of my forefather, the Prince
of Emghion, or Jemdjan, an Akritical Prince, that is
a Border protector on the Arab frontier, who was blinded
in Constantinople, in the Vlacherne Caverns, under the
reign of Nikiforos Votaniates. It is my greatest poem
of love and Passion. I cannot touch it nor see it because
I grow ill, when seeing this blind and tortured man.
(I must have somebody else to copy it for me, maybe Ekner,
maybe you.) Nobody else could have done it in Europe
but me. And this is not boasting. As you said on a
postcard, (the reverse of which I knew well, a protecting
Canopy Goddess), vain glory has no good position with
me. I absolutely cannot comprehend but that someone
has written with me as a medium (skrivit genom mig). I'd
like to send it to you and have it published in English
first but do not dare to touch it nor see it for a couple
months. Not vain, but proud. Still perfectly normal
and without a headache.

Really, I have never had such an experience, or, not
one so complete.

I am between East and West, a self-made Prince. And
one who has it as a heritage or Fate. I am what's really
noble - what is it? I'm half a noble, half a man, half
an artist, etc., and the opposites of all those, almost
whoever you may choose, almost, because I do not want to
out-bishop Bishops nor to out-whore whores, for instance.
Not even to out-Middle the Golden Medium. There is another
scale of temperature, (illegible), and Measure. I'm anti-
Goethe as well as anti-Nietzche but pro-Mozart.[21]

Auden never seemed to have any difficulties understanding what Ekelof had in mind with his rather ecstatic poems. As Ekelof wrote to me in a letter, explaining why he had become interested in the Byzantine, the Greek life: "Byzantine life, traditionally and according to deep-rooted custom, is like the political life in our cities and states.

I am intensely interested in it because I hate it. I hate what is Greek. I hate what is Byzantine..."[22] Auden's comment was: "I understand him (Ekelof) very well when he speaks of Byzantine life, both loving and hating it.'

Not until the work was done, and the translations were neatly typed up, did Auden raise the question of a publisher. How right he was when he warned against working "on spec", because when I offered the manuscript to major publishers the answers were disappointing, stating that "we here after careful consideration have come to the conclusion that we are not the right publisher for this verse". This time the difficulties were not insurmountable, to be sure, but when Ekelof's **SELECTED POEMS**[23] appeared, published first by Penguin in 1971, then by Pantheon in 1972, Ekelof had already numbered among the dead for several years. He died on March 16, 1968. If there was any British review of the book, we never heard of it; however, there was a sprinkling of encouraging, favorable, reviews in professional American journals - and without fanfare the beautiful volume was soon remaindered in New York at Marboro bookstores for $1 - where, I hope, some poetry lovers finally may have picked it up and enjoyed it. In London the Penguin edition of Ekelof is still in stock, fortunately. The commercial success of Hammarskjold - staying on the National Bestseller List for almost a year, selling half a million copies in hardcover in the U.S.A. and thousands in hardcover and paper in Britain and still selling, - and the relative commercial failure of Ekelof's poetry in the English-speaking world, could hardly have formed a greater contrast.

Since Auden had given his readers the benefit of more than 1,700 lines on the insights which his quotes, etc., were supposed to communicate, was I correct in assuming that Auden's **NEW YEAR LETTER**[24] (1 January 1940) contained the most extensive notes of explanations given by any poet in the English language? "No", he said, "that honor belongs to David Jones", referring to **THE ANATHEMATA**,[25] approximately one third of which is devoted to the notes, i.e., roughly 80 pages of the book. Eliot, as we know, commented on some of the lines in "The Waste Land", and later he expressed himself on the effect of his footnotes and explanatory notes: "But authors' notes (as illustrated by "The Waste Land") are no prophylactic against interpretation and dissection: they merely provide the serious researcher with more material to interpret and dissect."[26] Nevertheless, certain poets, including Empson,[27] Richards,[28] and others, have felt compelled to footnote their poems.

But why had Auden more or less given up on providing notes for his readers? "I realized that the poet's task is great enough, without footnotes and explications." For this reason the notes were completely excluded from the latest editions of his collected poems.

Reasonably familiar quotations of wit or insight are likely to add to the pleasure of the reader, whether or not this was the author's intention. The reader with strong scholarly inclinations will look up the source and make observations, preferably after having considered the full context of the quotation. But if it is time-consuming enough to look up "familiar", i.e. half-remembered, quotations, it will be so much more demanding to locate totally obscure quotations, especially if they are "hidden". When the "hidden" quotations are in English, French, German, Italian and/or Spanish, somebody educated in a traditional manner might enjoy the challenge of trying to identify them. If the suspect "hidden" quotations have an Eastern (Japanese, Chinese, or Indian) source - such as in Ezra Pound's **CANTOS** - they are complicating factors indeed, and there is an obvious need for an authoritative commentary. If the writer in an Eastern language were to employ 'hidden' quotations, Eastern and Western readers alike would require a commentary, and the Western reader - so unknowing about the treasures of Eastern literature - would need a translation as well, if such were to be found! From a purely practical, translator's point of view, if a text with "hidden" quotations is to be accurately translated into other languages, it is of paramount importance that all the details about the quotes be found.

It would be presumptuous to try to predict the shape of things to come, but it seems probable that there will be an increase in the use of quotations of all kinds. Since the tasks ahead for the humanities are multiplying at a rapid speed - while public support is being reduced - it would not be unreasonable to insist that authorized explanatory notes accompany any "learned" poem or prose poem, so that in the future we do not with increasing frequency find ourselves bogged down in an unmanageable mass of unidentified quotations. Our Western ignorance of the literatures of the world is such that we need a great deal of help in orienting ourselves towards more global horizons. What is, or should be, more than an intellectual amusement, could conceivably deteriorate into drudgery if readers were overwhelmed by too many unfamiliar quotations - a sad prospect, since there is no longer any accepted canon of works or any "orthodoxy" of literary conventions. Johnson's claim that "every quotation contributes something to the stability or enlargement of the language" might be more to the point if it were rephrased to read: not every quotation contributes to the stability of the language - confusion might also be the result! The poet's own notes might save us all in the end.

NOTES
1 **VAGMARKEN** (Stockholm, 1963), p. 73; **MARKINGS** (London/New York,1964), p. 90.
2 **EVENING LAND/AFTONLAND** (London, 1977).
3 "Encounter 17:5 (November 1961), pp. 3-4.
4 **MARKINGS**. On p. xxii, Auden calls Hammarskjold 'a great, good, and lovable man'.
5 When **VAGMARKEN** (1963) appeared as a Delfinbok (Stockholm, 1966), a substantial notes section had been added pp. 181-8.
6 16 August 1956; **VAGMARKEN**, p. 108; **MARKINGS**, p. 136.
7 **VAGMARKEN**, p. 112; **MARKINGS**, p. 141.
8 **VAGMARKEN**, p. 164; **MARKINGS**, p. 203.
9 **THE ENGLISH AUDEN. POEMS, ESSAYS AND DRAMATIC WRITINGS 1927-1939**, edited by Edward Mendelson (New York, 1977),p.170.
10 **VAGMARKEN**, p. 70; **MARKINGS**, p. 85.
11 Bonniers Operabibliotek (Stockholm, 1961). Cf. Staffan Bergsten, **OSTEN SJOSTRAND** (Twayne's World Authors Series 309) (New York, 1974), pp. 69-70.
12 Letter from Gunnar Ekelof, 17 April 1964.
13 **KRITISKT 40-TAL**, edited by Karl Vennberg and Werner Aspenstrom (Stockholm, 1948), pp. 282-304, and "Gunnar Ekelof - A Contemporary Mystic", translated by Robert Bly, **ODYSSEY REVIEW** (New York), 2 (1962), 238-56;

excerpts in **I DO BEST ALONE AT NIGHT, POEMS BY GUNNAR EKELOF**, translated by Robert Bly (Washington, DC, 1968), pp. 44-50, and in **FRIENDS, YOU DRANK SOME DARKNESS: THREE SWEDISH POETS, HARRY MARTINSON, GUNNAR EKELOF AND TOMAS TRANSTROMER**, chosen and translated by Robert Bly (Boston, 1975), pp.158-63.
14 (Stockholm, 1960). Auden, p. 51.
15 Letter, 17 April 1964.
16 Letter, 21 April 1964.
17 Letter, 21 April 1964.
18 Gunnar Ekelof, *Selected Poems*, edited by A. Alvarez and N. Stangos (Penguin Modern European Poets, London, 1971), pp. 38-40.
19 **SELECTED POEMS**, p. 42.
20 **SELECTED POEMS**, pp. 140-1.
21 Undated annotation in pencil on the front and back of a reprint from **GERMANIC REVIEW** (March 1965). The English is that of Ekelof, except for a few words supplied by me.
22 **SELECTED POEMS**, p. 10.
23 As Robert Bly has pointed out, the book is somewhat mistitled, "since it includes poems only from two very late books of the Byzantium trilogy" (**FRIENDS, YOU DRANK SOME DARKNESS**, p. 71). The choice of title was made by the editors.
24 (London, 1941 and 1965).
25 (London, 1952).
26 T. S. Eliot, a note of introduction in David Jones, **IN PARENTHESIS** (1937) (New York, 1961), p. vii.
27 **COLLECTED POEMS** (New York, 1948), in which pp. 87-113 contain the author's notes.
28 In **THE SCREEN AND OTHER POEMS** (New York, 1960), pp. 88-101 contain the notes.

ON TRANSLATING SONGS

Ruth Rubin

A singable translation of a foreign song is a poetic, idiomatic, easily sung set of seemingly original English lyrics, conveying the sense and emphasis of the original and precisely matching the metrical pattern of the music. The following is an elaboration on this thesis. The professional translators and scholars quoted were not thinking specifically about song translation but their remarks also apply thereto.

John Ciardi, in 1954, remarked on "translatorese...that queer language-of-the-study that counts words but misses their living force." Drawing attention to the very language of translation, instantly recognizable as inferior to the level of the original, translatorese makes a song a flop. What, then, is successful translation?

"A translation must be...read with ease and pleasure," or "it will never be read," says Theodore H. Savory in **THE ART OF TRANSLATION**, perhaps the best book on the subject.

> "The too brief and dogmatic statement that a translation must read like an original may be supported by a show of reason. The original reads like an original; hence it is only right that a translation of it should do so too; from the translation alone it should not be possible for the reader to determine whether it had been translated from French or Greek, from Arabic or Russian."

But is it really possible to convey in translation some of the feeling and flavor of a foreign folk song? I feel it is. Here are some of the considerations involved in arriving at a satisfactory translation.

If the songwriter doesn't know the foreign language in which a favorite song is written, someone else gives him a word-for-word translation. This he studies until "the author's intent hangs naked in the translator's mind," as Denver Lindley, author of **THE EDITOR'S PROBLEM**, puts it. "It has shed its original clothes and has yet found no new ones. The translator, a little like Edna St. Vincent Millay's

Euclid, looks on meaning bare."

In **THIRD THOUGHTS ON TRANSLATING POETRY**, Jackson Mathews discusses the same phase but is thinking primarily of poetry. We have only to substitute "song" for "poetry" in Mathews' comments. The translator, he says,

> "may misread his model in a number of ways: he may not see what is to be seen nor hear what is to be heard in it. But if he does see and hear clearly and fully, he will hold the original poem in a sort of colloidal suspension in his mind - I mean a fluid state in which the syntax, all the rigid features of the original dissolve, and yet its movements and inner structures persist and operate. It is out of these that he must make another poem that will speak, or sing, with his own voice."

In **FROM FRENCH TO ENGLISH**, Justin O'Brien describes four steps, including the one described above by Lindley and Mathews that, for him, make up the act of translating. Again, we have only to apply what he says about translating poetry to translating songs and to grasp how the song translator works. "First," he writes, "I read and reread the text as a whole to absorb it, and as it were, make it part of myself. Secondly, I write out the best version I can make, after weighing all possible alternatives that come to mind." The song translator does the same, noting how ideas mesh with the music, and how well the words sound, sing, and fit the material pattern of the music.

O'Brien tells us further:

> "Thirdly, after putting the first version aside for a time, I come back to it and read it through without reference to the original, making changes wherever necessary. The final translation must stand on its own. In the fourth place and as an ultimate precaution, I check the resultant second version with the original text, the details of which I may have by then happily forgotten, just to catch any passage

where I may have deviated too far from the text. Even with such cautious checking and rechecking, errors will persist..."

The author points out that a translator's faults may sometimes be due to the ambiguities of the text; I agree. Sometimes it is difficult to figure out what a passage means, or to find an equivalent expression or word in English. "Sometimes," says O'Brien, "the most difficult passages to put into English are the deceptively simple ones."

How is one to judge whether a song translation succeeds? Let's return to Mathews:

> "The final test of a translated poem must be does it speak, does it sing? In spite of the restrictions under which he works, in spite of his sense of fidelity to another poem, a translator is bound to sound out for himself. The poem he is writing is also his own. In it he is obliged to take over, to give a sense of command, to make his creative will felt. His instruments are style and his own voice. These can set him free to compose. The model, if it is to be translated, simply has to take the consequences of being transmuted into another voice, which is its new life. Every saddened reader knows that what a poem is most in danger of losing in translation is its life."

What does one do about those ideas which seem impossible to translate? Writes William Arrowsmith in **THE LIVELY CONVENTIONS OF TRANSLATION,**

> "...Before such apparent impossibilities, all translators are equal — though some are more equal than others. But the crucial requirement is tact: first, the tact of discretion by which the translator distinguishes between what is difficult and what is impossible; and second, the tact of skill with which he improvises before impossibility. Nothing more effectively dooms a

translation than the failure of the translator to improvise when confronted with transparent impossibility, or the converse, the habit of improvising before what is merely difficult."

These departures, according to Savory, should be "correct in idiom, expression and structure, but not more than this."

An example of improvisation or invention in the face of apparent impossibility may be cited from my own experience. I tried very hard to translate all the rich meanings of the word "lechem" in "Lomir Ale Zingen", but without success. I at first gave the word up as impossible, thinking to translate it simply as "bread". Finally, the brainstorm: retain the Yiddish word, which sings so well! But this in turn made it necessary to explain for Americans the meaning of it, which I did, by surrounding the word of the source language: "To a rich man, lechem means a white roll. But to us poor folk, oh, down-and-out folk, Lechem is a dry crust of bread." (**TREASURY OF JEWISH FOLKSONG**).

In "Translating from the German," Edwin and Willa Muir also comment on the need for invention when translating. "How to translate poetry, where the actual words, the music, and the movement signify so much more than they do in prose, I find it hard to understand. The verse translator obviously must be allowed far more freedom (including freedom to invent) than the translator of prose."

No translation, of course, is ever finished: as Valery said of poems, it can only be abandoned. This applies to folk songs too. If a translation is good enough to sing, it may very well be improved upon by the folksingers who pick it up. In the face of this likelihood, one "finishes" a song reluctantly.

If my own translations have any merit, they owe much to this reluctance to "finish", and to the many singers who pick up where I leave off, thus "finishing" a song for me.

SOME PROBLEMS IN TRANSLATION

Paul Forchheimer

To translate is defined in **THE CONCISE OXFORD DICTIONARY** as expressing the sense of a text in another language. This definition applies well to factual texts, especially scientific ones, but more is required for literary texts and, especially, in poetry, where it is important not only to convey the meaning correctly, but also to imitate the peculiar style and flavor.

Some problems, however, are common to all kinds of texts due to the different ways of the original language and the target language, all the more so if different cultures are involved.

The problems result from the nature of the vocabulary, of the grammar, and of the idiomatic expressions for which there are not always equivalent ones, yet the prosaic translation of which changes the character of the text.

As to vocabulary, it must be said that the exact meaning of a word is usually only determined in context (other than for precise scientific terms), and even then sometimes ambiguities arise. The various connotations of a word are usually different from language to language, if not from dialect to dialect. Picking a wrong equivalent in the target language can be misleading. Students who wrote essays in German on their plans after finishing college looked up the word "graduation" and found one equivalent, namely *Gradeinteilung*. The fact is that there is no equivalent concept in German, and *Gradeinteilungans* means graduation as in graduated cylinder, i.e. marks for measuring. Thus it is important before using an unknown word to check on its definition. Often a circumlocution or description is needed.

The translator must never be influenced by the similarity of words. The French word *chauffeur* used to mean primarily a stoke of a vehicle, but only rarely a driver of a motor vehicle, while in English it means a professional driver, and in German any driver. The German *trapez* means a trapezoid, but not a trapezium, yet it could also mean a trapeze. Thus not only cognates, but also common borrowings have often assumed different meanings. This applies even more to descriptive terms. German *Schwarzbeere* is blueberry, while English black berry is Brombeere in German. While German *Friseur* and Scandinavian firsor, (hairdresser, barber), obviously are of French origin, French has no such noun, and *friser*, while it can mean to curl, sometimes is translatable as to come close to.

Cultural differences show, too, in terms for colors and in kinship terms. While all people with normal eyes see similar colors and shades, some languages in Africa distinguish only four basic colors. Different lines on the spectrum are used for the standard colors, everything else being shades. Thus, while we distinguish between green and yellow, these are only shades of the classical Greek *chloros*, a yellowish green, which also gave the name to the halogen chlorine. Latin *avunculus* (whence our uncle) refers only to a maternal uncle. In Eskimo languages, paternal and maternal relatives are different concepts with different words. Older and younger brothers, also of father and mother, have different designations.

Grammatical differences pose some difficulties, as well. For example, German pronouns distinguish three genders. A relative pronoun then refers to the last antecedent of the same gender, while in English it would only refer to the very last antecedent. For this reason it is often necessary, in translation, to revamp the whole sentence. Yet this might obscure other relations and must be done with great care. On the other hand, English distinguishes animate and inanimate in who and which, and while this has some analogy in French, there is no such mechanism in German. These considerations are of special importance in scientific texts, patents and legal documents, where every word and implication is subject to scrutiny by legal experts. Here it is important to convey the exact meaning while excluding any unintended possibility of inference. Style is hardly of consideration here.

The French possessive *son*, *sa* agrees with the gender of the possessed, while the English his, her agrees with the gender of the possessor. If the context does not offer any clue, guessing can be dangerous. The only way out left would be to render in English "his or her", an awkward expression that should be avoided in a normal text if at all possible, but it is still better than a wrong guess. The German possessive agrees with both possessor and possessed.

For the translation of literary texts, the translator should have feelings akin to those of the author, or else he must be extremely versatile. Not only must he express the exact meaning of the original, he must also preserve as best as possible the style and flavor of its text. Often an author plays on words. An equivalent in the target language must be found, or else some of the flavor is lost. Elegant idioms which do not have a literal equivalent must be replaced carefully to preserve style and meaning. A plain prosaic translation would change the character.

Even more difficult is the translation of poetry. Besides maintaining the meaning, style and flavor, it is also important to retain the rhyme, rhythm and meter, yet the language should flow naturally and not appear forced. Here a natural gift is a great asset, if not a prerequisite, though time and effort are still indispensable.

Greater difficulties arise in translations into languages of a very different culture, especially a so-called primitive one. Here it is difficult to find equivalent words. While we classify animals by anatomic and physiological criteria, certain Australian cultures classify them into edible and non-edible animals. In a paper presented in 1988 at the City University of New York Graduate School, Eugene Nida of the American Bible Society discussed the difficulties of translating into languages of peoples in different cultures, where literal translations, if possible at all, would convey a completely false meaning. Similes would not be understood, moral values are different, and our standards of conduct make no sense. Yet the same difficulty had been faced by the early missionaries in Europe. New words had to be borrowed or freshly coined by loan translation for concepts which must first be taught to be understood, e.g. the term almighty or omnipotent. Often texts have been rewritten in the cultural frame of the people, as is the case of the Old Saxon *Heliant*. To the extent that objects or animals are unknown, a change of meaning can occur. Thus the Old High German word *helfant* (elephant) means a camel.

In a way, this problem is not much different from one in modern times. Every new term associated with a new theory, a new discovery, or a new invention must be explained and taught to be understood. This is also very important in the frequent cases when commonly-used words are used technically, endowed with a new, specific technical meaning.

An interesting situation was faced by this author when he was in charge of translations at the European Headquarters of Engineers Intelligence. On the one hand, the authors had to appear as good nationalist Germans, using artificial German coinages for current foreign words normally used in German. On the other hand, the use of foreign words was a sign of education. In a research paper on infrared radiation the professor had to use new German terms. But he also owed it to his academic standing to employ the established international scientific terms. Thus, a strange mixture resulted, and it was only possible by careful study of the text to decide whether two terms were fully synonymous or stood for different shades of meaning. Similarly, military papers of an army interpreter, given to us for translation, contained the normal German word for interpreter, *Dolmetscher*, a word of Slavic origin, and the artificial coinage *Sprachmittler*, language mediator. Did these terms, perhaps, stand for different military ranks, or was it merely a blend of old military tradition with required nationalistic purism? I decided for the latter.

But translations from languages associated with primitive cultures into European languages are also delicate. The very cultural background confers on the text a primitive character in European eyes. This is compounded unjustly by the condescending attitude of the translator. To the native the original text is serious and normal, but the translation often gives it a childish character. To do justice to the text requires much discretion.

THE TRANSLATOR AND THE MULTILINGUAL TEXT:
Two versions of Umberto Eco's NOME DELLA ROSA

FRITZ G. HENSEY

Umberto Eco's first novel, **IL NOME DELLA ROSA**, (1980) was a best-seller both in the Italian original and in at least two translations, namely William Weaver's English version (1985) and the Spanish version by Ricardo Pochtar (1984). Two salient features of **IL NOME DELLA ROSA** that challenge the translator are its rich intertextuality and its multilingualism.

Eco's later commentary (Postille) to this, his first novel... see Weaver's (1984) English version... concerns itself with intertextual aspects that start with the title itself and go on up to the medieval Latin verses that bring the work to its conclusion. Our own essay will address the second issue, that of the novel's frequent use of Latin and other languages. We will discuss how translators into somewhat different languages deal with such heterolingual elements, i.e. those not in the novel's basic language, Italian.

The vast majority of non-Italian passages are in some form of Latin: Classic, Vulgar, or mixed with Romance vernaculars. There are a few passages in Old High German, a fair number in one or more in Romance languages, and still others in regional or archaic forms of Italian. Since these passages have in common their being in a language other than the standard Italian of the novel as a whole, they will be called second language (L2) elements.

A great many of them are quotes or allusions contributing to the novel's overall intertextuality. More generally, multilingual narrative and dialogue help enhance the atmosphere of a 14th-century monastery in northern Italy. The plot is that of a Sherlock Holmes mystery, featuring Guglielmo di Baskerville and his assistant, but not quite Doctor, Adso(n).

In his essay on multilingualism in literary texts, Meir Sternberg (1981) argues that translators of such texts have a twofold task. First, there is a message to be decoded or carried over from the source language, SL, into a target language, TL. The author uses a certain national linguistic code, and via translation becomes, in effect, an author in a second national language code. Simultaneously, however, the very choice of medium has its own communicative functions, the more obviously so when some of the work's textuality is based on extensive use of third languages.

As far as the linguistic code is concerned, a translation into a second code may more or less accurately convey the message in a form culturally acceptable to the readership. For a given reading public, several of the languages used may be less accessible than the author assumed was the case of the original readers.

Language and cultural differences may oblige the translator of multilingual works to produce a version more linguistically homogeneous than the original. Only by observing the original may the critic discover what was lost in the translation as far as choice of medium is concerned. The average reader, however, would simply be deprived of a major dimension of the novel. Fortunately for both critic and ordinary reader of English or Spanish, both translators have certainly striven to avoid such loss.

Aside from his wide use of textual allusions, Eco achieves an added intertextual dimension by making substantial parts of the novel partially dependent on L2 passages. Translators sensitive to form as well as to content are apt to attempt to imitate such features of the source text using the resources of the TL and relying on a sense of what would be accessible to the readers of the version. While any translation may be considered in some sense mimetic, that of multilingual texts offers quite specific translation problems that can be approached in a specific fashion.

Sternberg proposes a scale of mimetic translation procedures ranging from overt transcription of heterolingual elements to their total effacement by conventional rendering into the target language. Such idealized extremes reflect a long-standing issue in translation theory: whether the translator's orientation or "loyalty" should be toward the source text, language, or author or to the target text, language, or reader.

Peter Newmark's (1988) recent translation textbook discusses the various forces that pull translators in several directions at once. Newmark's basic distinction between communicative and semantic approaches to translation speaks to the source-versus-target dichotomy.

Similarly, our own studies of multiple versions of the same text (Hensey 1982, 1984a, 1987, 1989) classifies common translation techniques as to how they relate syntactic and semantic patterns between source and target texts. The present essay proposes mimetic approaches using somewhat different linguistic resources and involving different cultural assumptions.

The comparative stylistics approach to translation, originally propounded by Vinay and Darbelnet (1953) and applied to Spanish/English translation by Vasquez-Ayora (1977), provides us with a useful point of departure. In this approach, one sets up units of translation based on the surface structure of the original.

While there are many criteria for treating a certain segment of the text as a unit of analysis, syntactic analysis into phrases and clauses is a common practical approach. Our observation of L2 elements in **NOME DELLA ROSA** leads to their classification on the basis of three syntactic patterns or levels: Phrase, Clause, and Text.

By noun phrase (NP) we understand a grammatical unit consisting of two or more words, one of which must always be a noun serving as nucleus or main element in the phrase. The noun nucleus is recognized, inter alia, because in the languages involved this is the element with which any modifying words must agree in gender and number. The same term is used here to include prepositional phrases. Units of this size are listed below as Phrase-Level units.

By clause we mean a set of two or more words, one of which must always be a verb serving as the nucleus of a verb phrase (VP). The verb nucleus is that element which must agree with the NP subject, expressed or understood, in person and number. The basic VP may or may not be accompanied by a subject NP as well as by other clauses. Thus, what we are calling clause quite often amounts to a full sentence. Units of this size are termed Clause-Level units.

An L2 passage consists of two or more conjoined sentences constitutes a text. In **NOME DELLA ROSA**, many such texts are fragments of poems, biblical passages, classical aphorisms, and other writings, mostly in Latin or a medieval Romance language. Figure 1 displays a set of examples in each category, randomly excerpted from Eco's original and identified by their page location and listed as Text-Level units.

Figure 1
SECOND-LANGUAGE (L2) ELEMENTS

<u>Phrase-Level Units</u>:
milier amicta sole (243)   ***   coram monachos (43)
***intus et in cute (283)   *** minimas differentias
odorum (247) *** vis appetitiva (246) *** supra
speculum (321) *** di paidikoi, di efebikoi e di
gynaikoi (24) *** su er thronos viginti et quattuor
(320)

<u>Clause-Level Units</u>:
verba vana aut risui apta non loqui (287) *** aut
semel aut iterum medium generaliter esto (283) ***
non in commotione, non in commotione Dominus (496)
*** er muoz gelichesame die leiter abwerfen, so er
an ir ufgestigen (495) *** vade retro (246)

<u>Text-Level Units</u>:
Est domus in terra, clara quae voce resultat. Ipsa
domus, etc. (128) *** oh sidus clarum puellarum,
etc...(249) *** age primum et septimum de
quattuor...in finibus Africae, amen (431) *** stat
rosa pristina nomine, nomina nuda tenemus (503)

Returning to Sternberg's scale of procedures for the translation of L2 elements, we see that the translator may come closest to the ST by simply transcribing those elements. For Sternberg's "selective reproduction" we choose the term <u>transcription</u>, which is illustrated in the examples of Figure 2. Both Weaver and Pochtar repeatedly transcribe L2 passages both long and short.

Figure 2
TRANSCRIPTIONS OF L2 ELEMENTS
ENGLISH VERSION

ECO: "oh langueo", gritai, e "Causam languoris video nec caveo!", anche perche un odore roseo... (p. 249)
WEAVER: ...and I cried, "Oh langueo", and "CausamU languoris video nec caveo", also because a rosy perfume etc. (p. 292)
ECO: ...strumenti di navigazione per cui le navi vadano unico homine regente, e ben piu rapide di quelle ... (p. 25)
WEAVER: instruments of navigation by which ships will proceed unico homine regente, and far more rapid than those etc. (p. 11)

SPANISH VERSION
ECO: Per cui naturalmente amor fecit quod ipsas res quae amantur, amanti aliquo ecc. Infatti io ora vedevo ... (p. 283)
POCHTAR: En virtud de lo cual, naturalmente, amor fecit quod ipsae res quae amantur, amanti aliquo etc. Enefecto, en aquel momento veia etc. (p. 342)
ECO: Guglielmo arrossi vivamente e commento: "Eris sacerdos in aeternum". "Grazie", disse l'Abate. (p. 42)
POCHTAR: Guillermo se cubrio de rubor y comento: — Eris sacerdos in aeternum. — Gracias — dijo el Abad. (p. 46)

Sternberg's "linguistic leveling" consists of treating the L2 element as if it were one more segment in the source language, i.e., by translating it. Since we have been using the term translation in a general sense, we will call such linguistic leveling <u>transcodification</u>. Figure 3 presents examples by Weaver and Pochtar. The first examples from each translator are transcodifications. We may note Pochtar's questionable translation of <u>traete</u> ("pull") as <u>entrad</u> ("come in").

Figure 3
<u>TRANSCODIFICATIONS OF L2 ELEMENTS</u>
ENGLISH VERSION

ECO: aliquando praeterea rido, jocor, ludo, homo sum (p. 138)
WEAVER: sometimes I laugh, I jest, I play because I am a man (p. 150)
ECO: graecum est, non legitur (p. 171)
WEAVER: Graecum est, non legitur...It's Greek to me. (p. 192)

<u>SPANISH VERSION</u>
ECO: traete, filii de puta (p. 431)
POCHTAR: entrad, hijos de puta (p. 520)
ECO: Pensano di e note come l'omo schernisca. (p. 271)
POCHTAR: Dia y noche piensan come burle al homine (p. 328)

The second examples show mixed procedures. Weaver first transcribes <u>graecum est, non legitur</u> and then follows up with an idiomatic English rendition. Pochtar's treatment is more complex.

First, we note that the source utterance is in a mixture of Latin and other Romance languages. We will hereafter refer to this usage as

Synthetized Romance Vernacular (SRV). Pochtar's version faithfully reproduces Eco's basic meaning: "Day and night they think of how to deceive men". Part of this translation is in Pochtar's own SRV which mixes Italian, Spanish, and Vulgar Latin. This treatment links what is mostly a transposition to the last of our procedures, transcreation.

Sternberg cites structural conversion and concept simulation as mimetic procedures focused respectively on grammatical and semantic features of the L2 element. Both of them amount to recreations of the source text by means of a purportedly equivalent target-language L2 element. Figure 4 displays this form of translation, which we choose to call transcreation. All the sample passages are in SRV, and the translators produced their own SRV renditions. Weaver shows somewhat more reliance on Latin and Italian, while Pochtar blends Italian and Spanish. Both mix their transcreations with transcodifications, but of the two, Weaver is the more prone to expand on the original.

Figure 4
TRANSCREATIONS OF L2 ELEMENTS
ENGLISH VERSION

ECO: Oc! Bestiola parvissima est, piu lunga alguna cosa che 'l topo, et odiala 'l topo muchissimo. (p. 311)

WEAVER: Oc! Parvissimum animal, just a bit plus longue than the rat, and also called the musk-rat. (p. 370)

ECO: Cave el diabolo! Semper m'aguaita in qualche canto per adentarme le calcagna. ma Salvatore non est insepiens! Bonom monasterium, et aqui se mangia et se priega dominum nostrum. Et il resto valet un fico seco. (p. 54)

WEAVER: Cave el diabolo! Semper lying in wait for

Continued...

Figure 4, cont'd.

> me in some angulum to snap at my heels. But Salvatore is not stupidus! Bonum monasterium, et aqui refectorium and pray to dominum nostrum. And the resto is not worth merda. (p. 47)
>
> SPANISH VERSION
> ECO: Cave basilishchium! Est lo reys dei serpenti, tant pleno del veleno che ne riluce tuto fuori! Che dicam, il veleno, il puzzo ne vien fuori che te ancide! (p. 311)
> POCHTAR: ;Cave basilischium! ;Est lo reys de las serpientes, tant pleno de veneno que reluce todo ppor fuera! ;Que dictam, el veneno, el hedor que solta ti mata. (p. 376)
> ECO: Oh, femena che vendese come mercandia, no po' unca bon essere, ni aver cortesia. (p.271)
> POCHTAR: Oh, femena que vendese come mercandia non puede numquam ser bona ni tener cortesia. (p.328)

Transcription and transcodification stand at opposite ends of a scale running from total acceptance of heterolingualism to its total denial. Transcription looks directly at the source text, transcodification at the target language. Between these two extremes, transcreation attempts to look in both directions at once: the translator wishes to preserve the passage's heterolingualism but finds it necessary to recast it into a dynamically equivalent form. For a fuller discussion of transcreativity and its application to literary forms like the sonnet, see Hensey (1984b).

Both translators use all three procedures, and it is appropriate to ask whether the choice of procedure varies significantly from one target language to the other. A reasonable hypothesis would be that since Latin is more accessible to speakers of Spanish than to those of English, Pochtar might show a greater tendency to transcribe rather than to transcodify.

For the same reason, it would appear much easier for the Spanish translator to imitate SRV passages. Many Romance languages are to some extent mutually intelligible, particularly in written form. Another possibility is that either of the translators may show a marked preference for one or the other of the procedures according to the grammatical level of the unit translated. A text would seem more apt to require transcodification ("straight" translation) than a clause, and the clause more so than the phrase.

Figure 5 displays the distribution, between the two translators, of 100 randomly selected segments of Eco's text considered as units of translation. There were 88 segments in Latin, 8 in synthetic Romance vernacular, three in German, and one in Greek. The units of translation are broken down by syntactic classification and by the procedure each translator chose for his rendition of that unit. A series of hypotheses were tested for significance by Chi-square. Because 88 of the 100 segments were in Latin, no attempt was made to make comparisons between source languages.

Figure 5
DISTRIBUTION OF PROCEDURES FOR TRANSLATING L2 ELEMENTS
(N = 100 units of translation)

WEAVER, THE NAME OF THE ROSE

UNIT LEVEL	TRANSLATION PROCEDURE			
	OMISSION	A	B	C
PHRASE	0	10	2	5
CLAUSE	2	18	8	6
TEXT	4	36	4	5
totals:	6	64	14	16

Chi-Square = 9.26, p = .159 n/s

Continued...

Figure 5 cont'd.

POCHTAR, <u>EL NOMBRE DE LA ROSA</u>

UNIT LEVEL	TRANSLATION PROCEDURE			
	OMISSION	A	B	C
PHRASE	0	16	0	1
CLAUSE	0	27	3	4
TEXT	0	45	0	4
totals:	0	88	3	9

Chi-Square = 6.77, p = .148 n/s

On totals only: Chi-Square = 18.8, p ,.001, sig.

A: TRANSCRIPTION   B: TRANSCODIFICATION
C: TRANSCRIPTION

Three null hypotheses were tested:

H1. There is no significant difference in Weaver's choice of procedure according to the type of translation unit involved.

H2. There is no significant difference in Pochtar's choice of procedure according to the type of translation unit involved.

H3. There is no significant difference between Weaver and Pochtar as regards their choice of translation procedure, regardless of size of translation unit.

The Chi Square test for significance was applied to each translator's table of procedures, and the results are displayed on Figure 5. The distribution of procedures according to syntactic level did not prove to be significant for either translator. Hence, the first two null hypotheses could not be rejected. When the test was applied to the totals, comparing the choice of procedures from one version to the other, a high level of significance was indicated. The third null hypothesis was rejected. The conclusion is that the two translators differ significantly in their choice of procedures independently of the type of translation unit involved.

The most frequent procedure by far was simple transcription, accounting for well over half of each translator's rendition of L2 texts, mostly in Latin. Pochtar was significantly more inclined than Weaver to reproduce the original. Conversely, Weaver was much more inclined to translate heterolingual elements into English, i.e., to transcodify. Weaver, too, was somewhat more prone to re-creating ("transcreating") such elements. On the whole, and judging from this limited sampling, Weaver's English version shows a more balanced choice of procedures.

Multilingual texts present translators with a challenge that may be met in several ways, all of which represent some form of mimesis. The procedures used can be described in an objective fashion, whether the critic's intention is a descriptive or comparative one. Studies of this nature can be useful in bringing the discussion of literary translation more in line with the increasingly scientific thrust of contemporary translation studies.

REFERENCES

Eco, Umberto. 1980. **IL NOME DELLA ROSA.** Milano: Gruppo Editoriale Bompiani. Translations: see Weaver (1985) and Pochtar (1984), below

Hensey, Fritz. 1982. "Consideraciones estructurales en la traduccion de `La pell de brau' de Salvador Espriu". In M. Duran (ed). **ACTES DEL SEGON COL.LOQUI D'ESTUDIS CATALANS A NORD-AMERICA.** Barcelona: Publicacions de l'Abadia de Montserrat.

____. 1984a. "Catalan poetry in translation: an experiment in applied interlinguistics". **HISPANIC LINGUISTICS** 1.1:41-56.

____. 1984b. "Palimpsests, transforms, and the presence of the original". in D. Jackson and A. Lefevere (eds.). **THE ARTS**

AND SCIENCE OF TRANSLATION. Dispositio 8.19-21:229-38
____. 1987. "Differential stylistics and alternative versions of a Garcia Marquez story": in T. Morgan et al., (eds.), **STUDIES IN SPANISH PHONOLOGY, SOCIOLINGUISTICS, AND APPLIED LINGUISTICS.** Lanham, MD: University Press of America, p. 317-37
____. 1989. "Dos versiones portuguesas de los Piimata de Constantino Cavafis". **HISPANIC LINGUISTICS** 2.2:299-320
Newmark, Peter. 1988. **A TEXTBOOK OF TRANSLATION.** Hempstead, UK: Prentice-Hall International
Pochtar, Ricardo. 1984. **EL NOMBRE DE LA ROSA.** Barcelona: Editorial Lumen, 9a edicion
Sternberg, Meir. 1981. "Polylingualism as reality and translation as mimesis". **POETICS TODAY** 2:4, 221-40
Vasquez-Ayora, G. 1977. "Introduction a la Traductologia". Washington, D.C.: Georgetown University Press
Vinay, Jean P. and Darbelnet, Jean. 1953. **STYLISTIQUE COMPAREE DU FRANCAIS ET DE L'ANGLAIS.** Montreal: Beauchemin
Weaver, William. 1984. Umberto Eco: **POSTSCRIPT TO NAME OF THE ROSE.** Translated by William Weaver. San Diego: Harcourt-Brace-Jovanovitch
____. 1985. **THE NAME OF THE ROSE.** New York: Warner Books, primera impresion. Edicion anterior en 1983 por Harcourt-Brace-Jovanovitch, NY

TRANSLATION: THE PROBLEM OF PURPOSE

RICHARD E. BRAUN

"Translations are a problem for us," the editor of a great Canadian press writes me, "since they are often not susceptible of consideration following our standard procedure, which is to get reports from two or more competent scholars, or other authorities." She concludes:

> passions rage over translations in a way in which they do not rage over anything else, and thus the obtaining of an adequate picture of a particular translation and its value can be difficult.

If Americans read closely, they will perceive, through the conventions of northern over- and understatement, a familiar message of dismay; they may call their act of perception criticism, analysis, or even translation. But recollecting the truisms of literary scholars regarding paraphrase, they will not be surprised at the dismay. Rather, they may be puzzled that they have understood the Canadian text so well.

We have heard that "form is meaning," and that poetry "is what is lost in translation." Useful statements, these, in special circumstances. The first might be used as a rejoinder to the vulgarian who asks a poet "Why can't you just say what you mean?" It might lead to explanations of the play aspect of literature, to reminders of the contrived suspensefulness of the book one can't put down, or to analogies with the styles of sports commentators. So too, the second: ethnic flavor and local atmosphere are quickly recognized as perishable elements of style. "And style," the clincher might run, "is the only difference between an Englishman and a Frenchman."

So much for that. But now comes the dictum of an eminent scientific investigator:[1]

> Phonemic similarity is sensed as semantic relationship. The pun, or to use a more erudite, and perhaps more precise term — paronomasia — reigns over poetic art,

and whether its rule is absolute or limited, poetry by definition is untranslatable. Only creative transposition is possible: either intralingual transposition — from one poetic shape into another, or interlingual transposition— from one language into another, or finally intersemiotic transposition — from one system of signs into another, e.g., from verbal art into music, dance, cinema, or painting.

These words are welcome to some esthetes, bred in schools which declare that the purpose of poetry is to perfect its own form.[2] These words seem to place on a foundation of firm learning what the *litterateur* had supposed was only the reaction of a freer and more sensitive generation against the classical prescription that poetry is meant to delight and to instruct.

The classicist, though — and I here affirm that that is what I try to be[3] — is prepared to argue for a conservative interpretation of Jakobson's "creative transposition." "Transposition" assumes that there exists something to be transposed. "Creative" need not imply falsification of that something. Moreover, the literature of linguistics, semantics, and communication theory does furnish the troubled republic of letters with better hope than the dictatorship of the pun.[4] The distinction between the meaning of forms, discoverable in their grammatical and contextual positions within a given language, and substance, is a confirmation of what we have believed since the time of Etienne Dolet. Meaning, in terms of situation, is goal-directed; meaning is purpose, and may be transmitted by a translation equivalent appropriate to the real-life situation. Languages differ more in what they must specify than in what they can.

This recognition — of the difference between meaning as a property of language and as the effective purpose of utterances — permits Professor Jakobson to qualify himself so gracefully. From a view of poetry as an exquisite, frivolous and frail art, where ambiguity is supreme, he goes on to assume, with gusto, that poetic content, the poetic message, the meaning, is sturdy enough to thrive through imitation, translation, and worse. One tends to feel vindicated. There must be something beyond its own, perfected form to a poem if it is to survive such rough use. If, after Berlioz, Pasolini, and Europe's acres of canvas, Vergil, Sophocles, and Ovid have not scattered into a cloud of "culture," surely Dryden and Humphries and Copley, Yeats and Fitts and Fitzgerald, Golding and Sandys and Gregory did not all delude themselves when they decided that the Latin and Greek had substance which English would not dissipate.

Plus ça change ... Dryden's categories, metaphrase, paraphrase, and imitation, fit well in this context.[5] The first is designed to help people learn a language: it is when commonly faced with the foreign text, and equipped with marginalia that the translator invites scrutiny of the untranslatable paronomasia, impossible chiasmas, and alien allusion. But all this paraphernalia is in pursuit, finally, of subject matter, even as is a bilingual dictionary. The third category, "imitation," also presupposes an animating purpose in or behind the original poem, and presumes that it is worth one's changing the text, cutting, expanding, and inventing in order to make this motive spirit perceptible to readers in a strange place or time. The middle ground, where critical passions most rage, seeks to compromise; but whatever liability it incurs by trying to stand as the honest broker, the aim of the "paraphrase" is to communicate the content of the original "sense for sense," as Jerome has it, "not word for word."

It will be clear by now that I am proposing (1) that the function of a translation is to transmit the message of the original, the content; (2) that the level at which form and content are not identical, but related, in the classic sense, as wine to its bottle, is normally the highest level. This is not to suggest that the esthetic layer is insignificant, but that it is, in the major genres at least, supportive rather than paramount. Condensation, inflation, euphony, simile, conceit, are devices of communication, tools in the task of delight and instruction. The meaning of the work is its final cause; the purpose of the translation should be that of the original.

Now, in this age of relativism, I know of but one serious attempt, in the West, to describe the purpose of poetry, that of Yvor Winters.[6] Poetry, he says, is artistic literature written in verse. Artistic literature is writing which "endeavors at one and the same time to clarify a subject rationally and to move the emotions appropriately:

> A poem (or other work of artistic literature) is a statement in words about a human experience.... THE ILIAD,

MACBETH, and "To the Virgins to Make Much of Time" all deal with human experiences. In each work, there is a content which is rationally apprehensible, and each work endeavors to communicate the emotion which is appropriate to the rational apprehension of the subject. The work is thus a judgment, rational and emotional, of the experience — that is a complete moral judgment in so far as the work is successful... We regard as greatest those works which deal with experiences which affect human life most profoundly, and this criterion is not merely one of the intensity of the experience but of the generality or inclusiveness of the implications.

I shall not analyze this statement, which is wonderful in its clarity. I should add, though, that within the domain of artistic literature Winters includes materials which apply to humbler mental processes than complete moral judgment. The passage quoted makes it clear that Winters regarded human experience as interesting in itself: value is implicitly attributed to "human interest." The communication of ordinary personality, as in the domestic novel of Wharton, is a worthwhile, if not a great subject.[7] Second, he admits a further worthy form of curiosity, which I may call "factual interest," satisfied in historiography and the Melville novel by details which, "since we are gentlemen and scholars," we find interesting.[8] At best, literature orders and judges, fitting emotion to fact; but even at less than best, it satisfies a hunger for knowledge, that is for vicarious experience.

If, then, the purpose of poetry is rationally to communicate experience with the appropriate emotion, the purpose of translation is to communicate that same subject and emotion. The problem of the literary translator is how to execute the job of communication. That is a problem of literary quality; for, as Winters warns, "a work which is poorly executed is bad, no matter what the conception."[9]

There are translations, noted translations, which are so far removed from the purpose of the original, that I would be glad of a new term to describe them. "Imitations" will not do; for those are compositions which depend on fidelity to the spirit of an original. Possibly "impressions" will suit the case, since the authors stamp their model with new, often special or personal meaning.[10] "Parody" is the ancient word; but its present connotations are wrong. Writers of impressions usually love and respect the original.

It would be unfair to criticize an impression — Lattimore's **ILIAD**, for example — as a bad translation: as unfair as to criticize the **AMERICAN STANDARD REVISED BIBLE**. The latter is full of unintelligible "translatorese," in the manner of a metaphrase in a bilingual edition. Yet many people would reject Phillips' translation, or one like, precisely because it communicates the content of the original in correct, clear English. These people, feeling that the subject matter of religion by nature contains much that is mysterious, much that is magical, regard the cryptic Standard Version as more authentic. The argument that the Gospel is a vital message, meant to inform and to move, will be regarded as impertinent by such an audience. (After all, what is the ministry for?) The congregation demands distortion because of its heartfelt faith.

The **ILIAD**, it seems, is no longer regarded as a sacred text. Lattimore's distortions, nevertheless, serve a quasi-sacerdotal purpose: affective obscurantism. The character of the audience, here too, is paramount.

Now Homer is the creator of the Greek language. Like the itinerant poets of Arabia, he blended dialects into a national literary medium. He is a champion of useful language. Accordingly, the **ILIAD** and **ODYSSEY** require translation into the freshest and richest modern English. However, observe:

> These then putting out went over the ways of the water
> while Atreus' son told his people to wash off their
> defilement
> And they washed it away and threw the washings into the
> salt sea.
> Then they accomplished perfect hecatombs to Appollo,
> of bulls and goats along the beach of the barren salt sea.
> (**ILIAD** I, 312-16)

This is not translation of any recognizable type. Its speech is not natural English, or its style effective as English style; but neither is it mere "translatorese." It is less a work of literalism than a contrived impression, which achieves a special emotional accompaniment to the material: a new emotion, foreign to Homer. Lattimore's purpose is to arouse nostalgia in a particular audience. For, those who once studied Greek, and read some Homer, and were called away by other pursuits, will respond to Lattimore via the memories he invokes: the old feeling of working one's way through the original aided by Keep's English translation of Autenrieth's Homeric dictionary, the satisfaction of winning ease with the idiom and of learning about ancient religious practices — all this at a time of life where vigor is high and whatever is strange is exciting.

The sanctity of past youth has made Lattimore's the Standard American **ILIAD**. Its odd phrases and sentence structures function much like the poignant snippets of Homer and Horace in Norman Douglas' **SOUTH WIND**, where echoes of schoolboy and scholarly pursuits counterpoint more severe themes. Thus, false to the emotion of the original, Lattimore substitutes wistfulness, and so abandons the possibility of communicating Homer's "complete moral judgment."[11] However, I repeat, it is foolish to censure an author for not accomplishing what he never intended. Even in a radical "impression," many of the original's values may be communicated. So, Lattimore transmits, to the intellect, the narrative movement of Homer's **ILIAD**, its historical information, its measurement of the gulf between men and immortal gods, and the exposition and delineation of fate and free will. That is, Lattimore, like Homer, feeds the hunger for knowledge.

Another famed impression is Zukofsky's translation of Catullus. I have written elsewhere that this book is not meant to communicate Catullan logic and feeling, but induce readers of Latin to learn more English.[12] It is addressed to learned literati. The Zukofsky Catullus can do nothing but good — to the intellect — and for this reason: through most of its history, English has been formed by bilingual authors: men whose Latin was as good as their Anglo-Saxon, then by those whose French was better, and then, again, by men who had spoken only Latin in their Tudor-and-later grammar schools; and it is important for us as scholars to experience this state of mind once more, to practice approaching the chaos of English, living and changing, from the reliable base of Latin. But let me specify here, too, that the Zukofsky impression has human interest: one's curiosity gathers something of Catullus' personality — the false innocent, the good hater, the experimenter in disparate levels of discourse.

If, then, such free creations, where one poet alters the emotional, another the rational order of a model, bring over worthwhile material from the source, what is to be expected of orthodox paraphrase translations? The critical cruces, and the crises of poetic strategy are even more obvious when the methods are less radical. The problems of intent and content remain those of audience, especially when the cultural difference is great.[13]

One of the persistent problems in translation of Greek and Latin classics is the suitable treatment of passages of strong emotional content. Ancient Greeks and Italians felt that sincerity or intensity of emotion is in a direct ratio to the amplitude of its expression. This is the opposite of present-day feeling in the English-speaking nations.

Few would deny that the Fourth Book of Vergil's **AENEID** is a well-executed clarification of delusive amorous passion; that it applies to this content the correct emotions of anguish, pity, and regret; that it is tragic because it is public and great because it applies generally to mankind. Yet, it is a work which, today, in English translation, as often embarrasses as convinces. Take, for example, Anna's discovery of Dido's suicide. Here is a situation to move us. A Canadian or American Anna would probably say no more than:

> Dido? ... Dido!
> My God ...

She might say nothing — on stage, or on the page, as well as in life. The English signal of sincerity is silence. But see how Anna begins (675-9):

> Hoc illud, germana, fuit? Me fraude petebas?
> Hoc rogus iste mihi, hoc ignes araeque parabant?
> quid primum deserta querar? Comitemne sororem
> sprevisti moriens? Eadem me ad fata vocasses:
> idem ambas ferro dolor atque eadem hora tulisset.

Reading the beautiful Latin verse — accepting, with it, the values of

Roman tradition — one believes, and to some degree feels that the emotion Vergil conveys is appropriate to the situation.

But read a good English prose rendering:[14]

> O Sister, so this was the truth? You planned to deceive me! Was this what your pyre, your altars, and the fires were to mean for me? How shall I begin reproaching you for forsaking me so? Did you scorn your own sister and not want her with you when you died? You should have asked me to share your fate, and then one same hour, one agony of the blade, might have taken us both.

The same content becomes excessive, tedious. Turn, then, to one of the finest modern verse versions:[15]

> Dido, was this what it meant? You lied? to me?
> Was this the purpose of pyre, altar, and flame?
> You left me! What shall I say? You died, but scorned
> to take me? You might have let me share your death:
> one hour, one stroke of pain had served for two.

This is decent compromise. It stresses the feeling, and omits qualifications. It cuts twenty syllables from the count of the original, where the prose version added twelve.[16] But, in the garb of normal syntax, plain English diction, and modern-stage blank verse, this version would need to be pared still more in order to convince us — that is, to cause us to share the emotion. These lines succeed in communicating the fact that the emotion was real. This half-success itself appeals to the underlying unity of mankind; for a characteristic of all peoples is the realization that the styles of all peoples differ.

Finally, to demonstrate, by contrast, the severity of the strictures on emotional expression which our present, puritan language imposes on the classical translator, I would like to exhibit the same passage in the common idiom of Restoration heroic drama:[17]

> "Was all that pomp of woe for this prepar'd;

> These fires, this fun'ral pile, these altars rear'd?
> Was all this train of plots contriv'd," said she,
> Which is the worst? Didst thou in death pretend
> To scorn thy sister, or delude they friend?
> Thy summon'd sister, and thy friend, had come;
> One sword had serv'd us both, one common tomb..."

Again, as with Vergil's ornate, rhetorical Latin, we are persuaded of the propriety of the emotion within its cultural context. Volubility of emotional expression is perfectly at home in the now-obsolete tradition of stage-rant. Today, however, if judged by the standards applied to Copley's translation, Dryden's would be condemned as frigid exaggeration, which not only keep us from sharing the emotion, but forbids our approving it as credible.

For the taste of his day, Dryden effected a creative transposition; and it may be said, too, that Copley began but stopped just short of achieving a parallel adjustment for our day. What should he have done? To have written, as suggested,

> Dido? ... Dido! ... My God ...

would have turned the translation from paraphrase into imitation. No, given the cultural gap, Copley made the logical and honorable choice.

Here, we are faced by another epigram:[18]

> Because it (translation) is always a compromise, and
> great art is rarely a compromise, the odds are against it.

This admonishment goads us, in the quest of masterwork, to cross the barrier between paraphrase and imitation. If we must omit passages to satisfy the temporal or national spirit, may we not also insert others to gain the same end? Again, there comes the support of science.[19] Communication theory suggests that the message should be made to fit the decoder's channel. Otherwise, there is a communication overload, and for two reasons: because in translation the normal redundancy of the source language is lost, and because the audience of the source message was provided with circumstantial information which the receptor-language audience lacks. The translator is obligated to provide redundancy to match the original; and, when an idea or image is implicit in the source language, he will usually have to make it explicit in translation. How far this process of adjustment may go will define the boundary between paraphrase and imitation.

The problem is commonly a subtle one. The imitator is, after all, not nearly so radical as the impressor.[20] For the author intending paraphrase, the border of imitation may not be clearly marked. As an example of the peril, I shall expose an effort of my own, the **RHESOS** of Euripides.[21]

At the turning-point of the play, the Chorus is trying to persuade Hektor to admit Rhesos as an ally. We, the audience, know that if Rhesos settles in Hektor's camp, he will die. Hektor does not know this, but is indignant because Rhesos has arrived so late in the war. "We've kept Troy safe without his help," Hektor says; and the Chorus, "Then you're convinced we've won?" Hektor answers:

> Yes, I am. And the daylight will prove I'm right.
> The gods will shine on us.

CHORUS

> Please sir,
> we can't know the future before we see it.
> The gods can change anything.

The Chorus' reply is a single Greek verse (332), which Lattimore translates:

> Look to the future. God often reverses fortunes.

Now, Lattimore was aiming to retain the simplicity of the **RHESOS**, an under-written play, terse, elliptical, allusive, which depends, for much of its impact, on an audience's knowledge of Homer and the cyclic poets. How am I to justify the fullness of my version? On the principle stated above: the need to fill out ellipses, and explain the implicit message, in order to avoid overload. "Please, sir" is added as functional redundancy, and to maintain the tone of a soldier addressing his superior — a small concession to the naturalistic mode of the English stage. The gnomic *"oed to mellor"* is changed into argument because it is part of a debate; the isolated, sententious phrase might be obscure in this context. "Know" is added to "see" (Lattimore's "look") because the play's main themes are knowledge and ignorance, perception and deception, and I felt the necessity of signalling this motif at this crucial position in the plot. The final sentence is virtually the same in both versions: it means, in metaphrase, "a/the god turns over many things." Thus far, my translation, like Lattimore's, is a paraphrase.

But then I began to think that "change" fell far below the potential suggestiveness of the image implicit in "turns over". "Turns over" what? Fortunes? Certainly. But, to me, "often reverses fortunes" is an Aristotelian gloss. So I sought a poetic gloss. Having observed that throughout the **RHESOS** Euripides associates the power of the Greeks with the sea and ships, and that of the Trojans with the land and the life of the soil, I decided that here, with the play's outcome about to be decided, was the time to write strongly: "Turn over ... the earth!" I wrote, seeing myself now as a "creative transposer,"

> Please sir,
> we can't know the future until we see it.
> Till then, a god can change it.
> We see the earth.
> Then a farmer cuts it, turns it upside down,
> and buries it. The place we know is hidden,
> and things from underneath are crawling in the light.

A bit much? I felt not. My three and a half intruded verses are in keeping with the themes and images of the play with the "motivating spirit" of the poetic structure. Here, a *deus ex machina*, the Oxford Press editor, showed me that I had transgressed the boundary between paraphrase and imitation. This is a perfect example of how such categorical borders come to be violated. Yet it had not appeared to me, when I did it, that I was shifting to a different literary mode; weeks afterward, I still had to be persuaded to make the logical and honorable choice.

Observe, too, that in my imitation, I not only expanded an implicit metaphor, but psychologized the passage: converted unconscious content into self-conscious awareness. This, again, typifies the imitator's device of introducing topicality. True, many have noticed, from the use of dreams, for instance, in Aeschylus' **CHOEPHORI** and Sophocles' **OEDIPUS TYRANNOS**, that the Greeks — possibly by way of the cult of Asklepios — had knowledge of what has come to be called Freudian psychology. Likewise, one hears the expression "pre-Freudians," used of such writers as Melville. However, the belief, even the certainty, that Greek tragedians used a similar system does not permit a translator (paraphraser) to emphasize his perception of this fact beyond certain bounds.

The trouble is that the bounds are not always certain. The trap of topicality is often hidden. It is the conservative critic who must serve distinctions which enthusiastic translators overlook. The procedures of committee translation which the United Bible Societies employ may be worth the consideration of literary translators who believe deeply in the value of their chosen authors.[22]

The appeal I have made to the human or humane content of major works does not invalidate Jakobson's remark about the reign of the pun over some literary genres. The epigram, the short lyric and conceited reflective poem are indeed less translatable than the epic, drama, or novel. Lacking plot, often without argumentation, the short forms are more elliptical and more dependent upon accidental linguistic features. The most important of these features is ambiguity. Translation equivalents, in cases of shared exponence and polysemy, occur only by coincidence.[23] Therefore, the dynamic-equivalent translation of these condensed yet fragile genres cannot be achieved by any single method.

Even in larger forms, the drama and satire, ambiguous words and excentric expressions, including proverbs, are sometimes employed to combine the experience with its proper emotion. Here, the translator may not elect not to proceed. He must compromise, Adams' remark notwithstanding, and hope for the best, trusting that the whole work cannot stand or fall by his choice.

Here again, I shall illustrate with my own work.[24] Verses 115-18 of Persius' *"Satire V"* read as follows:

> sin tu, cum fueris nostrae paulo ante farinae,
> pelliculam veterem retines et fronte politus
> astutam vapido servas in pectore volpem,
> quae dederam supra relego funemque reduco

They may be literally translated thus:

> But if, though just a while ago you were of our flour,
> you retain your old hide; and if, though your forehead
> is smooth, you're hiding a sly fox in your stale chest;
> if so, I'm taking back what I gave you before, and
> drawing back the rope.

None of this means much to the English reader. None of the Latin means simply what it says. It is a wild mixture of metaphors and proverbs. It is also an extreme sample of Persius' characteristic literary tactics: for Persius generates glee, his concept of the suitable emotional accompaniment, while exhorting to virtue. So, here, he treats a segment of an earnest sermon joyfully, as a comic extravaganza. The passage is actually a warning, and might have been expressed in such sober prose as:

> If you are a sincere Stoic now, and successful in your
> moral self-reforms, I will acknowledge that you have
> really changed, have freed yourself from the bonds of
> folly, and I will greet you accordingly, as a free man and
> an equal; if not, not.

That is explanation, not translation. To translate, I tried to substitute parallel exocentric expressions current in English:

> But if, though just a bit ago you flocked
> together with us, you've retained your old spots;
> or if you're wearing sheep's clothing to hide
> a sour grape; if so, I've given you enough rope.

This, left to itself, is risky. The feeling may be right; but what of the message? I decided I had no choice but to supply a metaphrase and expound it.[25]

Now, "to be of the same flour" refers to different grades which millers ground, the finer being the more costly; metaphorically, the expression means "to be of the same sort or quality," to share similar tastes, or to be devoted to like beliefs. The "old hide" is a piece of a proverb of the variety "Your fur is dyed, but the hide below is the same as before." The "smooth forehead" disguises a troubled heart or guilty conscience. The "chest" is where the heart is, but "stale" (vapido) refers to "bad wine in a good barrel." This image is distorted by mixture with the saying (Suetonius, **VESPASIAN**, 16) "the fox changes his fur, not his character." The introduction of a hidden fox further suggests the old tale (see Plutarch, **LYCURGUS**, 18.1) of the Spartan boy who stole a young fox and hid it under his coat and, rather than be detected in the theft, let the animal disembowel him; he stood thus in silence, and so died. The anecdote was repeated as a sample of the success of Spartan educational methods; but, in Persius' context, it comes to signify the self-destructiveness of concealing guilt. The "rope" figure in Latin does not imply suicide by hanging, but has to do with the vain efforts of an animal on a rope (compare "Satire V", lines 158-60) that strains and chokes itself, or goes too far and is dragged painfully back.

The success or failure of my Persius is, of course, a function of the judgment of the critical reader. That judicious reader may prove difficult to find. He may be someone as hard-pressed for reliable criteria as my Canadian editor, and say "translations are a problem for me." This is about what Johnson did in the famous discussion of 1778:[26]

> GARRICK. (to Harris.) "Pray, Sir, have you read Potter's Aeschylus?" HARRIS. "Yes; and think it pretty." GARRICK. (to Johnson.) "And what think you, Sir, of it?" JOHNSON. "I thought what I read of it verbiage: but upon Mr. Harris's recommendation, I will read a play. (To Mr. Harris.) Don't prescribe two." Mr. Harris suggested one, I do not remember which. JOHNSON. "We must try its effect as an English poem; that is the way to judge of the merit of a translation. Translations are, in general, for people who cannot read the original."

And, I must say, to be faced with such a trial, to have his translation judged as a poem, is not likely to give the translator courage. For now, unlike Johnson's day, passions rage over poetry in the same way as over translations.

Every writer who turns his taste or temperament to practice, is in danger of elevating his practice to principle. The same risk belongs to all of us who accept others' principles chiefly because they suit our habits of thought. I am describing common custom. The result is that the criteria used to judge of the effect of literary works are narrow and subjective.

It may now be time to begin cooperative, interdisciplinary efforts to establish principles of literary purpose and method that will have the force of reason. Only in this way can we hope to get reports from authorities who are competent to describe and evaluate translations. But this course of discovery demands greater seriousness than the average writer, scholar, and scientist appears, today, to possess. It demands high commitment to values of life, and belief in the fundamental unity of knowledge.

ENDNOTES

1 Roman Jakobson, in Reuben A. Brower, On Translation (Harvard Studies in Comparative Literature 23, Cambridge, Mass., 1959), 238.

2 An attitude found, for instance, in R. S. Crane, **THE LANGUAGES OF CRITICISM AND THE STRUCTURE OF POETRY** (Toronto, 1953), 60, 155.

3 I take the term "classicist" — commonly misused as a synonym of "classical scholar" — as a praise word (like "Christian") which signifies one who strives to embody, in life and letters, the abiding spiritual and cultural values of Greek and Roman civilization.

Addendum, 1990: today I would agree <u>in toto</u> with Jakobson's statement, and deny the feasibility of "paraphrase" in the translation of poetic texts, where only "creative transposition" is, indeed, possible.

4 See Joshua Whatmough, **LANGUAGE** (New York: New American Library, 1956), Ch. 5, especially pages 75-7; Eugene A. Nida, Towards a Science of Translating (Leiden: E. J. Brill, 1964), Chs. 3-6; and J. C. Catford, A Linguistic Theory of Translation (London: Oxford University Press, 1965), Chs. 5-7.

5 "Metaphrase" corresponds to the linguist's "formal equivalent," both "paraphrase" and "imitation" to "dynamic equivalent" translation. See Nida, op. cit., Ch. 8, especially 161-71.

6 I condense here an abiding principle of Winters, codified in "Problems for the Modern Critic of Literature," in **THE FUNCTION OF CRITICISM** (London: Routledge & Kegan Paul, 1962), 40.

7 Ibid., 30-1.

8 Ibid., 40-1.

9 Ibid., 27. Let it be specified that Winters regarded the conventions of "imitation" as obstacles to consistently good writing, and evidence of the inferiority of the major poetic forms, epic, tragedy, comedy.

10 In defense of multiplying terminology, I should point out that in current teaching practice the word "metaphrase" is applied to direct word-for-word and form-for-form transfer, such as this of John 1:6-7 (cf. Nida, op. cit., 186):

> became/happened man, sent from God, name to-him John;
> this-one came-he into testimony/witness
> that testify/witness-might-he about the light
> that all believe-might-they through him

"Literal": (Dryden's "metaphrase") is used of versions in the range of the Revised Standard Version:

> There was a man sent from God, whose name was John.
> He came for testimony,
> to bear witness to the light,
> that all might believe through him.

Another suitable word for works that step beyond the definition of "imitation" might be "descant." The old practice of inscribing "After Homer" or "After Catullus" below the title was a signal that an impression or descant was to follow. But it was sometimes used of imitations and even paraphrases.

11   D. S. Carne-Ross, in "The Classics and the Man of Letters," (**ARION**, Vol. III, Number 4, Winter, 1964), 30 speaks of the contrast, which I take it is what the poem supremely offers, between the terrible circumstance of the story and what C. S. Lewis called "the unwearying, unmoved, angelic speech of Homer." The **ILIAD** envisions a depth of human suffering darker even than Lear, yet the language never loses its accent of joy and triumph, never ceases to glorify the human condition.

12   Richard Emil Braun, "The Original Language: Some Postwar Translations of Catullus," **GROSSETESTE REVIEW**, Vol. 3, No. 4, Winter, 1970, 27-34.

13   A useful discussion of strategies employed when ancient conventions are not viable, per se, in English is William Arrowsmith's "The Lively Conventions of Translation," in William Arrowsmith and Roger Shattuck, **THE CRAFT AND CONTEXT OF TRANSLATION** (Austin: University of Texas Press, 1961, 122-40.

14   W. F. Jackson Knight, Vergil, **THE AENEID** (London: Penguin Books, 1956).

15   Frank O. Copley, **THE AENEID-VERGIL** (New York: The Bobbs-Merrill Company, Inc., 1965).

16 I propose that the syllable is the honest measure of comparative length. Latin hexameters average fifteen syllables, English blank verse, ten; and the Latin and Greek words also are, on the average, longer than English. But the roots, relationals and endings of Latin and Greek, like the roots, conjunctions, pronouns, and auxiliaries of English, are of one or two syllables.

17 John Dryden, published in 1697. For the style of translations and their acceptability, see Reuben A. Brower, "Seven Agamemnons," in Brower, op. cit. (note 1), 173-95. Brower's main thesis is that widely-used translations are composed in the general idiom currently regarded as "poetic". Thus, (Ibid., 173-4):

> A reader quite familiar with Dryden will find it impossible to distinguish Dryden's own translations of Juvenal from those of his helpers...If you should   define the poetry of Pope or of Dryden from their translations alone, we should find we were omitting most of what distinguishes them from their contemporaries.

18   Robert M. Adams, **PROTEUS, HIS LIES, HIS TRUTH, DISCUSSIONS OF LITERARY TRANSLATION** (New York: W. W. Norton & Company, Inc., 1973), 179.

19 Nida, op. cit., 129-32.

20 Nor is the impressor necessarily so fully conscious of the degree of his radicalism as are some of Jakobson's intersemiotic transposers. Vivaldi and Tartini must have been aware of the conditions of transfer, being both poets and composers. **THE SEASONS**, of course, presents parallel arts in its sonnets and concerti. But the sonata **DIDONE ABBANDONATA** is still bolder abstraction; for here, Tartini proposes to convey the emotion appropriate to part of Aeneid IV without a jot of Vergil's rationally-apprehended content. The sonata may delight, but I doubt that Tartini thought it could instruct.

21 Richard Emil Braun, **Euripides' RHESOS** (New York: Oxford University Press, 1978).

22 See Eugene A. Nida and Charles R. Taber, **THE THEORY AND PRACTICE OF TRANSLATION** (Leiden: E. J. Brill, 1969), Ch. 8, and the Appendix, 174-88.

23 The success of Ezra Pound's adaptation of Catullus 26 is due to the fortuitous coincidence of Latin and English idiom: the polysemy of <u>oppositus ad</u> ("exposed to—" and "placed as security for a loan of—"), and "draft" happily correspond.

> This villa is raked of winds from fore and aft,
> All Boreas' sons in bluster and yet more
> Against it is this TWO HUNDRED THOUSAND sesterces,
> All out against it, oh my God:
> some draft.

24 Richard Emil Braun, **Persius' SATIRES**, (Lawrence, Kansas: Coronado Press, 1984).

25 The strategem — of providing literal translations and supplying cultural data in elaborate notes, to supplement a literary translation — was suggested to me by Abokov's Pushkin.

26 James Boswell, **THE LIFE OF SAMUEL JOHNSON LL.D.**, London, 1793 (the 6th ed. of Malone, reprinted, New York: The Modern Library, 1931), 784.

ON TRANSLATING

Martin Tucker

The other day a story written in English came into our magazine office with the title "<u>Entre les Endroits</u>". Underneath the French title was an English equivalent in parentheses: "Middle Ground." Nothing better exemplifies the pitfalls, infelicities and felicities of the art of translation than this small example. For while "middle ground" is certainly an extrapolation of the French phrase, it is not the only alternative along the linguistic way-station. And while it brings a certain focus, it also diminishes other possibilities of illumination. Translation is inevitably a choice of alternatives, and the choice not taken makes all the difference in what is left said.

The essential role of the translator is to find a medium, but not a mean and not the middle ground, through which to filter the original language and expression into its proper script. The immediate question that comes to attention is, "what is proper"? Is it more proper to be literal (and thus eschew a likely chance of misrepresentation of the actual words) than it is to attempt to gain the essence of a writer's word-views? To gain essence means to gain entrance into a writer's soul and body of expression, and this exposure of body and soul is what literature is all about. But how does one gain such entrance without risking the pitfalls of going one's own way? We are, after all, pervasively human enough to be self-centered at our core. And is it so safe from misrepresentation to take the literal path? Literalness produces meaninglessness, since words without nuance, without something beyond the literal, are shorn of their meaning; they come too close up to the reader's consciousness without giving him/her a perspective by which to see the object in view. One thinks of a similar word, littoral, that shore which is too close to provide a view of the expanse, but which provides a seeming shelter of near ground and shallow sea.

The questions here posed, basic to the art of translation, are the questions raised in the craft of any literary art. Meaning is found not only in words, but in the space beneath, above and between the words. The translator's job becomes infinitely more difficult when he attempts the heroic task of matching the original genius of a work in all its spatial affects with his own limited linguistic tools. If it is *hubris* to compare oneself with a master literary artist when one is translating the work of such an artist, it is yet a situation in which humility demands that the translator attempt his utmost to reach the height and depth of the original. For translation is a reach as well as a grasp—it is an approximation of the genius of the original rendered in humility, but crafted with all the tools one can put one's mind on. When the translator's work approaches the quality of the original work, then the translation may be said also to be a work of art. Such concomitances happen. Not always, and not frequently, but they do, and the result is a wonder to behold. One thinks of Edward Fitzgerald and what he made from Omar Khyam: another jewel in the crown of rubiyats. Fitzgerald did not always render Khyam accurately if accuracy is measured by transliteration of spare parts, lines and/or chapters of an epic, yet he connoted Khyam's vision and Khyam's unique sense of the acceptance of the world. No translation of the Rubiyat has come close to the impact Fitzgerald's version has made on the world; in the process, Fitzgerald's own artistry has been recognized as deserving of high honor and reputation. Translators from the Greek, ancient and modern, share a more crowded arena; each has its due, as readers of Robert Fitzgerald, Richard Lattimore, and Edmund Keeley, among others, show. When it comes to niceties of translation—to the *mot juste*, whether in Flaubert (who coined the phrase without thought of later translation; indeed the phrase is almost always rendered in its French sparing/sparring elegance), or to those following in the Flaubertian tradition—there is always Vladimir Nabokov and Edmund Wilson to fall on. And when it comes to the almost insuperable challenge of encapsulating the hot flood of feeling in Yiddish verse, or, inversely, to allow for a free-moving rhythm within the formal cadences of Hebrew rhetoric, one turns to several able writers/translators, such as Aaron Kramer, who show the feat can be done.

What then distinguishes a great translation from a good translation, or a good translation from a poor one? Distinctions are often lines drawn in sand (to purloin a phrase) which a new critical wind shifts away. But some base material remains, just as Ozymandias was not entirely obliterated in the sands of the desert, and just as ruins in Greece and Rome show structural strength, while their more painted and decorative features disappear into the face of oblivion. At **CONFRONTATION**, we read a great deal of translated material; about 20 per cent of the material received here is translated from any number of languages, including Greek, French, Italian, German, Hindi, Hebrew, Yiddish, Armenian, Russian, Polish, Portuguese, Spanish, including work from Latin American and the Caribbean, Hungarian, Bulgarian, Slovakian, Slovenian, Croatian, and Serbian, Swedish, Danish, and Finnish. Our readers know only a small number of these above-mentioned languages—certainly no one on our staff knows Finnish, though I have met several distinguished Finnish writers at P.E.N. Congresses. How are we to judge a work worthy of publication in our magazine?

Perhaps we should start with basic tenets of translation. Most of us agree it is cogent to speak of one translation of the **ILIAD** or **ODYSSEY** when making a comparison with another translation of the work; the merits of Robert Fitzgerald are sometimes placed side by side against those of Richard Lattimore. Yet most people refer to the **ILIAD** or **OEDIPUS REX** when they have not read either work in the original Greek but in a translation, and when they are not discussing translation *per se*. The habit is farflung and seen in many dresses (and addresses) of language. Partly this habit is the result of laziness and overload of the academic brain: a translator's name is one more cog to remember before a teacher can get to the wheel of response with his students. But I and all those who ignore the translator and this contribution, not out of animosity or prejudice but from sheer thoughtlessness, are continuing in a tradition endemic to democracy. The whole—the field of composition—seems to be what counts when a teacher or editor is trying to reach a captive and/or free audience. The aristocracy of merit of any one translator becomes submerged in the good for all the works translated in this process of evangelizing. It is, of course, difficult to reverse the democratic tide in the United States of the past two hundred years, a tide which shapes American culture as well as its history and social policies. Yet, recognizing a phenomenon, we can at least see how much translators have been slighted in the commonwealth of ideas.

I began my brief essay by stating that my experience with translation is neither a formal nor a professional one. I read translations for possible publication in a literary journal. My choices are sometimes erratic, for I try to be a creative reader, and such an effort demands subversion of the known at certain times and angles. If my behavior as a judge is anarchic—that is, not subject to codification—it is also consistent with what good translation does to the body it feeds upon. The following is how I, and our other editors, judge translation for **CONFRONTATION: A LITERARY JOURNAL:**

1. We read for content and meaning.
2. We read for style and grace.
3. We do not read for literal accuracy.
4. We make periodic checks on the original work being translated as we operate on our lay intelligence. We do not pretend a scholarly competence. When we deem a work to be questionable in its translation or adaptation, we call upon the services of professional linguists, critics, and colleagues.

What we look for in translation is what Robert Lowell called "adaptation"—that is, a work to stand beside the original as an inspiration for it and containing its breath, but not all its form and sinew. Taking this stance, each translation becomes a part of the original, not its whole, though it is indivisible from the original whole in any discussion of its literary matter. Because we see translation in this way, translation becomes for us the work of an artist in a contained but freely imaginative sphere.

THE MAKING OF ARTISTS: A TRANSLATOR'S WORK

Donald Gilzinger

The art of translation is inspirational and sublime, the practice of bibliography literal and unromantic. By definition, a bibliography must be accurate, intelligent, complete, and efficiently organized. How else may the writer's life and work be justly represented? How else will the words not be lost?

Aaron Kramer presents a unique challenge to a bibliographer. His writing crosses all boundaries of modern letters. One must be prepared to describe Aaron's own books; anthologies in which he has participated; contributions to journals and newspapers; radio programs; audio recordings and publications of his poetry and translations set to music; audio and visual recordings of poetry readings and lectures in libraries, in classrooms, or in special venues; films; libretti; manuscript material and much more. I know. I'm the bibliographer.

A significant facet of Aaron's art is his love of translation; therefore, a bibliography will mirror his lifetime respect for, among others, Yiddish and German poets. The select list that follows contains both print and nonprint items that demonstrate his commitment to translation. The citations are brief, but monographs Aaron wrote or edited receive a long description. This inventory can only suggest the range of his interests and abilities. The catalogue is far from complete, but it will guide you to Aaron's words. What better goal for bibliography?

SELECTED MONOGRAPHS WITH KRAMER TRANSLATIONS:
(in which Kramer is the sole or the principal translator or to which he contributes significantly)

THE POETRY AND PROSE OF / Heinrich Heine / SELECTED AND EDITED WITH AN INTRODUCTION / BY FREDERIC EWEN (ornament) THE POETRY / TRANSLATED BY LOUIS UNTERMEYER, HUMBERT / WOLFE, EMMA LAZARUS, MARGARET ARMOUR, / AND OTHERS, INCLUDING 110 NEW TRANSLATIONS / BY AARON KRAMER (ornament) THE PROSE / NEWLY TRANSLATED BY FREDERIC EWEN / THE

CITADEL PRESS NEW YORK.
21.5 X 14.5 cm. Published in 1948, at $6.00. Issued in black cloth and stamped in gold on front cover and spine. Front cover: signature of Heine. Spine: THE / POETRY / AND / PROSE / OF / Heinrich / Heine / EWEN / CITADEL. Dust jacket printed in blue, beige, white, and black. A reproduction of a portrait of Heine appears on the front of the dust jacket. 874 pages. All edges trimmed.
NOTE: Kramer translates 110 of the 162 poems in the volume, including the 508 quatrains of "Germany: A Winter's Tale."
NOTE: The poems translated by Louis Untermeyer are reprinted from Heinrich Heine: **PARADOX AND POET** (Harcourt, Brace & Co., 1937).
NOTE: Two complete paperback editions were later published.
NOTE: An abbreviated version, without the prose, was printed in paperback in 1969. Louis Untermeyer and Thomas Mann are quoted on the cover as follows: "The selection and translation are of equal / excellence." Thomas Mann / "It is the finest...collection of Heine that I / know." Louis Untermeyer.

Denmark Vesey / and other poems / including translations from the Yiddish / by / Aaron Kramer / NEW YORK / (dot) / 1952.
20 X 13.5 cm. Published in 1952, at $0.75. Privately printed in an edition of 1000 and issued in stiff grey paper covers. Stamped in black on front cover and spine. Front cover: DENMARK / VESEY / and other poems / (line) / by / Aaron Kramer. Spine: DENMARK VESEY / Kramer. 48 pages. All edges trimmed.
NOTE: Includes twenty-two translations of poems by Morris Winchevsky, Morris Rosenfeld, David Edelshtat, and Joseph Bovshover.

The Teardrop Millionaire / and other poems by / MORRIS ROSENFELD / selected and translated by / Aaron Kramer / WITH A CRITICAL EVALUATION by KALMAN MARMOR / AND A BIOGRAPHICAL SKETCH by AARON KRAMER / Published by MANHATTAN EMMA LAZARUS CLUBS / New York, 1955
20.5 X 13.5 cm. Published in 1955, at $0.35. Issued in stiff green paper covers and stamped in black on the front and back covers. Front cover:

the / teardrop / millionaire / and / other poems / (photograph of Morris Rosenfeld) / by Morris Rosenfeld / Selected and translated by / AARON KRAMER / Emma Lazarus Clubs of Manhattan. Back cover: Price 35 cents. 32 pages. All edges trimmed.
NOTE: Includes sixteen translations of Rosenfeld.
NOTE: Marmor's essay is excerpted from a longer work on Rosenfeld appearing in the volume **THE BEGINNINGS OF YIDDISH LITERATURE IN AMERICA** (YKUF, 1944) and is translated from Yiddish by Kramer.

"JEWISH LIFE" ANTHOLOGY, 1946-1956; A SELECTION OF SHORT STORIES, POEMS AND ESSAYS DRAWN FROM THE MAGAZINE. Editorial Board: Louis Harap and others. New York: Jewish Life, 1956. 51-58+
Twelve translations from Yiddish of Winchevsky, Rosenfeld, Edelshtat, Bovshover, Hirsh Glik, and Shmerke Katcherginski, and "Song of the Palmach," an anonymous poem from Hebrew.

Mickiewicz, Adam. **ADAM MICKIEWICZ: NEW SELECTED POEMS**. Ed. Clark Mills. New York: Voyages, 1957. 71-2.
Excerpt from "Jankiel's Concert" (in Book Ten of Mickiewicz's epic **PAN TADEUSZ**) translated from Polish by Kramer. Complete passage published as "The Concert of Concerts" in **THE POLISH REVIEW** Autumn 1956: 63-7.

Ronch, Isaac Elchanan. **SELECTED POEMS**. Translated from Yiddish by Ira Mark (i.e. pseudonym of Kramer), Max Rosenfeld, Ruth Rubin and others. Drawings by Mark Chagall. New York: Alliance, 1961. 11-13+
Includes eighteen Kramer translations.

Judine, Sister M., comp. **GOETHE TO IBSEN**. New York: Macmillan, 1962. 49-54.
Includes six translations from German which comprise the entire Heine section.

MOSES / Poems and Translations / AARON KRAMER / O'HARE BOOKS / NEW YORK
17.5 X 11 cm. Published in 1962, at $1.25 in an edition of one thousand copies. Library of Congress Catalogue Card Number 62-6598. Issued in green cloth without boards and stamped in black on the cover: MOSES / AARON KRAMER. Stamped in black on the spine: KRAMER / MOSES / O'HARE. 96 pages. All edges trimmed.
NOTE: Includes 47 translations from Yiddish of poems by Winchevsky, Rosenfeld, Edelshtat, Bovshover, Dora Teitelboim, Isaac E. Ronch, and Hirsh Glik. Also includes the "Ballad of Itzik Wittenberg" by Shmerke Katcherginski.
NOTE: "Before the Judge," part of Edelshtat's manuscript effects, was made available to Kramer by the poet's sister for translation from Russian.

goethe (dot) schiller (dot) heine / Songs / and / Ballads / translated by / aaron kramer / o'hare books (dot) new york city
21.5 X 14 cm. Published in 1963, at $0.50.
The edition was limited to five hundred numbered copies. Issued in stiff white paper covers and stamped in blue on the front cover. Front cover: goethe (dot) schiller (dot) heine / Songs / and / Ballads / translated by / aaron kramer. 32 pages. All edges trimmed.
NOTE: Includes twenty-five translations from German: ten of Goethe, two of Schiller, and thirteen of Heine.
NOTE: None of the Heine translations are included in **THE POETRY AND PROSE OF HEINRICH HEINE.**

MORRIS ROSENFELD: SELECTIONS FROM HIS POETRY AND PROSE. Edited by Itche Goldberg and Max Rosenfeld. New York: Yiddishe Kultur Farband, 1964. 26-29+
Includes fifteen Kramer translations from Yiddish.

Mandel, Sigfried. **RAINER MARIE RILKE: THE POETIC INSTINCT.** Carbondale, IL: Southern Illinois UP, 1965. 17+
Includes ten Kramer translations from German.

Plotz, Helen, comp. **POEMS FROM THE GERMAN**. New York: Crowell, 1967. 87+
Includes two translations from German of Heine. English and German on facing pages.

Rainer Maria Rilke: VISIONS OF CHRIST / (bar) / A Posthumous Cycle of Poems / edited, with an introduction, by Siegfried Mandel / poems translated by Aaron Kramer / University of Colorado Press (slash) Boulder
22 X 23.5 cm. Published in 1967, at $4.85. Issued in tan cloth, stamped in black on front cover and spine. Cover: Rainer Maria Rilke: VISIONS OF CHRIST / (bar) / A Posthumous Cycle of Poems. Spine: Rainer Maria Rilke: VISIONS OF CHRIST / MANDEL (ornament) KRAMER / COLORADO. Tan endpapers. 106 pages. All edges trimmed. Dust jacket printed in blue, black, and white.
NOTE: German and English texts printed on facing pages.
NOTE: Mandel's introduction includes and credits two additional Kramer translations from Rilke: 25 lines from an 1893 poem, "Christ on the Grass" (15-16), and a two quatrain 1896 poem, "To ———" (28).

Howe, Irving and Eliezer Greenberg. **A TREASURY OF YIDDISH POETRY**. New York: Holt, 1969, 78-80.
Includes three translations from Yiddish of Rosenfeld.

TEUTONIC LITERATURE IN ENGLISH TRANSLATION. Compiled by James E. Miller, Jr. and others. Glenview, Il: Scott, Foresman, 1970. 12+
Includes five Kramer translations from German of Heine.

POEMS / by / ABRAHAM REISEN / Translated by Aaron Kramer
23 X 15.5 cm. Published by Dowling College Press in 1971, at $0.75. Issued in an edition of two hundred copies in stiff light green paper covers and stamped in black on the front cover. Front cover: POEMS / by / ABRAHAM REISEN / Translated by Aaron Kramer. 28 pages. All edges trimmed.
NOTE: Includes thirty-six poems translated from Yiddish.

Peretz, I.L. Selected Stories. Ed. Irving Howe and Eliezer Greenberg. New York: Schocken, 1974. 41-48.
Includes Kramer's translation from Yiddish of the short story "Three Gifts."

Foner, Philip Sheldon, comp. **AMERICAN LABOR SONGS OF THE NINETEENTH CENTURY**. Urbana, IL: University of Illinois Press, 1975, 318-21.
Includes nine translations from Yiddish of Edelshtat, Rosenfeld, and Bovshover.

Howe, Irving. **WORLD OF OUR FATHERS**. New York: Harcourt, 1976. 420-22.
Includes portions of four translations from Yiddish of Winchevsky, Edelshtat, and Rosenfeld.

100 HUNGARIAN POEMS. Ed. Thomas Kabdebo. Manchester, Eng.: Albion, 1976. 55-6+
Includes two translations from Hungarian of Frigyes Karinthy and Tibor Tollas.

Heine, Heinrich. **HEINRICH HEINE: POETRY AND PROSE**. Jost Hermand and Robert C. Holub, eds. New York: Continuum, 1982. 13+
Includes fourteen Kramer translations from German, including the entire "Germany: A Winter's Tale" (232-97).

"Rochel Boimvol: a Half Century of Literary Creativity." **THE ISRAEL YEARBOOK 1982**. Tel Aviv, Isr.: Israel Yearbook Pubs., 1982. 314-16.
Includes six translations from Yiddish of Boimvol.

Kossoff, Philip. **VALIANT HEART: A BIOGRAPHY OF HEINRICH HEINE**. New York: Cornwall, 1983. 9+
Includes twenty Kramer translations from German.

Ewen, Frederic. **HEROIC IMAGINATION: THE CREATIVE GENIUS OF EUROPE FROM WATERLOO (1815) TO THE REVOLUTION OF 1848.** Secaucus, NJ: Citadel, 1984. 557+
Includes five translations from German of Heine.

Peter, Alan, ed. **ANTHOLOGY OF MAGAZINE VERSE AND YEARBOOK OF AMERICAN POETRY.** 1984 ed. Beverly Hills, CA: Monitor, 1984. 174-75+
Includes two translations from Yiddish of Jacob Glatstein and Jack Gordon.

NORTON ANTHOLOGY OF WORLD MASTERPIECES. Ed. Maynard Mack, et.al. 4th ed., v.2. New York: Norton, 1985. 418-20.
Includes two translations from German of Heine.

Schwartz, Chaim. **POEMS: TRANSLATED FROM YIDDISH.** Los Angeles, CA, Westland Printing Company, 1986. 5-8+
Includes eighteen Kramer translations.

OCARINA: FRESHNESS OF THE ANCIENT. Guest ed. Menke Katz. Ocarina's Double Annual 1986/87. Madras, India: Tagore Institute, 1987. 12+
Includes thirty-two Kramer translations from Yiddish.

A CENTURY / OF YIDDISH POETRY / Selected, Translated, and Edited by / Aaron Kramer / (publisher's device) / Cornwall Books / New York (dot) London (dot) Toronto
15.5 X 24 cm. Published in 1989, at $24.95. Issued in black vinyl over boards and stamped in gold on the spine. Spine: Kramer / A Century of Yiddish Poetry / (publisher's device) Dust jacket printed in grey, brown, black, and white. Front: A Century / of Yiddish Poetry / Selected, Translated, and Edited by / Aaron Kramer. Spine: Kramer / A Century of Yiddish Poetry / (publisher's device) Back: (photograph of Kramer) / About Aaron Kramer / (biographical sketch) / Cornwall Books / New York (dot) London (dot) Toronto. 368 pages. All edges trimmed.
NOTE: Contains 136 Yiddish poets and 371 translations as well as a biographical sketch of each poet.

TO COMMEMORATE THE WARSAW GHETTO UPRISING: A RECORD RECITAL OF YIDDISH SONGS. Ed. Manus O'Riordan. Dublin, Ire.: Irish Jewish Museum, 1989. 3-4+ Includes fifteen Kramer translations from Yiddish.

SELECTED PERIODICALS WITH KRAMER TRANSLATIONS:

"Poems of Morris Winchevsky." **JEWISH LIFE** May 1950: 23-25. Kramer's biographical sketch of Winchevsky of 23-24. Includes six translations from Yiddish.

"Poems of Morris Rosenfeld." **JEWISH LIFE** June 1950: 16-19. Kramer's biographical sketch of Rosenfeld on 16-18. Includes five translations from Yiddish.

"Poems of David Edelshtat." **JEWISH LIFE** July 1950: 12-14. Kramer's biographical sketch of Edelshtat on 12-13. Includes seven translations from Yiddish.

"Poems of Joseph Bovshover." **JEWISH LIFE** Aug. 1950: 14-16. Kramer's biographical sketch of Bovshover on 14-15. Includes four translations from Yiddish.

"The Last One, the First One." **THE CHICAGO JEWISH FORUM** Spring 1952: 206. Translation from Yiddish of Isaac E. Ronch.

"Four Women Poets." **JEWISH LIFE** Nov. 1955: 13-16. Biographical notes by Kramer on 13-14. Includes one translation each from Yiddish of Sarah Barkan, Sarah Fell-Yellin, Hannah Safran, and Dora Teitelboim.

"Fair." **ADELPHI QUARTERLY** Summer 1962: 85-9. Translation from German of Rilke.

"Venice." **UNIVERSITY OF DENVER QUARTERLY** Summer 1967: 111-14. Translation from German of Rilke.

"There Once Was a House." **THE POLISH REVIEW** Spring 1968: 58-62. Translation from Yiddish of Dora Teitelboim.

"Three Poems by Abraham Reisen (1876-1953)." **MIDSTREAM** June/July 1968: 63-4. Translations from Yiddish.

"Yiddish Poetry, the First Golden Age." **MIDSTREAM** Apr. 1970: 16-26. Includes many passages of poems in Kramer's translations.

"Three Translations." **MODERN POETRY STUDIES 2** (1971): 201+ Includes three Kramer translations from Hungarian of Erno Szep, Gyula Illyes, and Mihaly Babits.

(Three translations) **STREET 2** (1975): n. pag. Includes three translations from Hungarian of Istvan Simon, Tibor Tollas, and Frigyes Karinthy.

"The Emperor of Atlantis; or, Death Abdicates: a Legend in Four Scenes." **MIDSTREAM** Apr. 1975: 38-43. Translation from German by Kramer of the libretto by Peter Kien. Revised version premiered in 1977.

"New Translations of Ingeborg Bachmann (1926-1973)." **THE DENVER QUARTERLY** Spring 1976: 21-47. Fifteen translations from German of Bachmann's Die Gestundete Zeit. With Siegfried Mandel.

(Two translations) **NEW ENGLAND REVIEW** Summer 1982: 557-8. Translations from Yiddish of Jack Gordon and Jacob Friedman.

"Seven Yiddish Lullabies." **MIDSTREAM** Apr. 1983: 55-6. Includes seven translations from Yiddish of Michel Gordon, Mendele Moicher Sforim, Isaac Peretz, Sholem Aleichem, Simeon Frug, Abraham Liessin, and Hersh-David Nomberg. Kramer's introductory sketch on 55.

"Isaac Reingold, the Fifth Sweatshop Poet." **JEWISH CURRENTS** May 1983: 12-19. Nine translations from Yiddish and an introductory essay.

(Two translations) **CUMBERLAND POETRY REVIEW** Fall 1985: 29+ Two translations from German of Ingeborg Bachman. With Siegfried Mandel.

(Two translations) **WRITER'S FORUM** Fall 1985: 17-8. Translations from German of Ingeborg Bachmann. With Siegfried Mandel. German text included.

"The Crest of a Great Wave: Seven More Yiddish Proletarian Poets." **JEWISH CURRENTS** Jan. 1986: 26-32. Kramer traces the careers, and translates poetry, of Leon Zolotkoff, David Goldstein, Anna Rapport, Benjamin Rosenblum, Nahum Babud, Jacob Adler, and Joel Slonim.

"Three Translations." **MIDSTREAM** Apr. 1987: 49. Translations from Yiddish of Anna Margolin, Rajzel Zychlinska, and Rochel Boimvol.

"Soviet-Jewish Martyrs: August 12, 1952." **OUTLOOK** July/Aug. 1987: 12-3. Four translations from Yiddish of Peretz Markish, Itzik Feffer, and Leib Kvitko.

(Six translations) **BITTERROOT** Winter 1987/88: 10+ Translations from Yiddish of Yuri Suhl, A.M. Dillon, J. Papiernikoff, Joseph Rolnik, and B. Bialostotsky.

(Three translations) **VISIONS** #26 Winter 1988: (37) Three translations from Yiddish of Zychlinska.

"Translations From the Yiddish by Aaron Kramer." **BITTERROOT** Summer 1988: 49-65. Includes twenty-four translations of various poems.

(Five translations) **JEWISH CURRENTS** Oct. 1988: 14-7+ Translations from Yiddish of Joseph Kerler, Abraham Sutzkever, and Sholem Shtern.

(Four translations) **MIDSTREAM** Feb./Mar. 1989: 20+ Translations from Yiddish of Malke Heifetz-Tussman, Meyer Shtiker, and Abraham Sutzkever.

(Two translations) **CUMBERLAND POETRY REVIEW** Fall 1989: 56-61. Two hitherto unpublished translations from German of Heine.

"A Lullaby of the Holocaust." **JOURNAL OF HUMANISTIC PSYCHOLOGY** Spring 1990: 51-4. Kramer's historical essay about Yiddish lullabies introduces his translation from German of "A Cradle Song for Myself: the Song of a Seventeen Year Old" by Selma Meerbaum-Eisinger.

SELECTED RECORDINGS OF KRAMER TRANSLATIONS:
(all recordings, except as indicated other wise, are audiotapes)

Kramer, Aaron. Serenade by Aaron Kramer: Poets of New York. Kramer reads his own and others poetry including four translations from Yiddish of Rosenfeld. Folkways, FL9703, 1957. Phonograph record.

Heinrich Heine: Balladeer of the World. Kramer reads his translations of the ballads of Heine. WBAI, New York. 1 Jan. 1961.

Yiddish Resistance Poetry of World War Two. Kramer reads and discusses poetry written by members of the Jewish resistance and others during the Second World War. Most of the translations are Kramer's. WBAI, New York, 12 Mar. 1961.

Adam Mickiewicz. Kramer provides commentary and reads nine translations from Polish of Mickiewicz. The translations are those of Kramer, W.H. Auden, and Louise Bogan. WBAI, New York. 23 Apr. 1961.

The Role of the Hero in Old and Middle English Poetry. Also titled Six Battles. Kramer reads seven selections from Old English, Middle English, and Middle Scots poetry. He provides explanatory commentary on the poems. Translations of passages from The Bruce and "The Battle of Maldon" by Kramer. WBAI, New York. 2 July 1961.

Goethe in Translation. Kramer reads and discusses selections from Goethe including many of his own translations which he so identifies. Also includes translations by G.M. Cookson and Stephen Spender. WBAI, New York. 20 Aug. 1961.

Morris Winchevsky and David Edelshtat: Sweatshop Poets. Part One of the Sweatshop Poets Series. Kramer provides introductions and reads translations of eight poems by Winchevsky and seven by Edelshtat. WBAI, New York. 18 Nov. 1961.

Morris Rosenfeld: A Centenary Tribute. Part Two of the Sweatshop Poets Series. Kramer commemorates the 100th anniversary of the birth of Rosenfeld with an introductory discussion and reading of seventeen translations of Rosenfeld poems. WBAI, New York. 20 Jan. 1962.

Joseph Bovshover: Sweatshop Poet. Part Three of the Sweatshop Poets Series. Kramer provides commentary and reads translations of eighteen poems by Bovshover. WBAI, New York. 25 Feb. 1962.

Poetry of Heinrich Heine. Kramer reads twenty-two of his translations from German of Heine's poetry and provides commentary. A Spoken Words Program. WNYC, New York. 10 July 1962.

Songs and Ballads: Goethe, Schiller, Heine. Kramer provides commentary and reads seventeen translations of the German poets. KPFK, Los Angeles. Sep. 1963. Rebroadcast by WBAI, New York, 17 Oct. 1963.

Heine: The Poet as Prophet. Kramer provides commentary and reads ten translations from German of Heine. Transcribed by George David from a rebroadcast on KPFK, Los Angeles. WBAI, New York. 6 Nov. 1964.

Five Peace Songs. Includes the translation from German of "Prayer of the Children" by Bertolt Brecht. Set to music by Waldemar Hille. Sung by Arnet Amos, baritone. First Unitarian Church, Los Angeles. 5 Nov. 1966.

Abraham Reisen. Kramer describes the life and work of poet and short story writer Abraham Reisen. He reads in Yiddish, translates and discusses the story "Shabbes in New York," followed by the poems "Tsu a Shneyela" (To a Snowflake) and "Di Shevuoth." Kramer then reads his translation of the poem "On the Hill" and discusses the short stories "Es shokelt zich" (It's Shaking) and "Der amoliger Socialist" (The One-time Socialist). YIVO Institute for Advanced Jewish Studies, New York. 6 Mar. 1968.

Moshe Leib Halpern. Kramer describes the life and work of poet Moshe Leib Halpern, as well as the activities of "Di Yunge," an early twentieth century writers' group. Kramer reads in Yiddish, translates and discusses "Abie Curley" and "Ich hob doch gehat." He and Dr. Schlomo Noble of the YIVO Institute discuss Halpern's relationship with "In Zich," a writers' group noted for introspection and technical innovation. YIVO Institute for Advanced Jewish Studies, New York. 13 Mar. 1968.

Moshe Nadir. Kramer discusses the life and work of poet and satirist Isaac Reis, known as Moshe Nadir. He reads in Yiddish, translates and analyzes "Mama-loshen" (Mother Tongue) and "Heinrich Heine." Kramer also discusses the influence of Heine on the work of Nadir. YIVO Institute for Advanced Jewish Studies, New York. 3 Apr. 1968.

Abraham Sutzkever. Kramer discusses the life and work of poet and resistance hero of the Vilna ghetto Abraham Sutzkever. He reads in Yiddish and the last two sections of "Mein Mama" in his translation.

YIVO Institute for Advanced Jewish Studies, New York. 24 Apr. 1968.

Rilke: Visions of Christ. Kramer reads six selections from his translations from the German of Rainer Maria Rilke's poetic cycle. He also reads from Siegfried Mandel's introduction to Visions of Christ. A Spoken Words Program. WNYC, New York. 23 Jan. 1969.

Transition to the New World: Shop and Tenement. Kramer describes the lives and work of a number of Jewish writers who emigrated to the United States at the end of the nineteenth century. He reads his translations from the Yiddish of selected poetry and prose of Morris Winchevsky, David Edelstadt, Joseph Bovshover, Morris Rosenfeld, Z. Libin, and Abraham Reisen. YIVO Institute for Advanced Jewish Studies, New York. 23 Apr. 1969.

Morris Rosenfeld, Leon Kobrin, and Z. Libin. Kramer describes the life and work of Jewish immigrant writers and reads selections from Morris Rosenfeld, Leon Kobrin, and Z. Libin, pseudonym for Israel Hurvitz. Kramer also traces the emergence of Yiddish newspapers and the "Golden Age" of the Yiddish theater in New York. Introduction by Dr. Schlomo Noble of the YIVO Institute. YIVO Institute for Advanced Jewish Studies, New York. 15 Apr. 1970.

Kramer, Aaron. On Freedom's Side: The Songs and Poems of Aaron Kramer. With Viki Ann Diamond, Joan Fishman, and Karl Finger. Includes the translation from German of Heine's "My Poems ar Full of Poison," set to music by Irwin Heilner and performed by Fishman. Rec. 3 Mar. 1973. Freneau, FR10755, 1974. Phonograph record.

Schrogin, Joseph. The Music of Joseph Schrogin. With Estelle Marlow. "What is the World?" by Rosenfeld, translated from Yiddish. Katilansky Culture Club, c. 1975. Phonograph record.

Poetry of Abraham Reisen. Kramer provides an introduction and reads a selection of his translations from Yiddish of the poetry of Reisen. A Spoken Words Program. WNYC, New York. 20 May 1975.

Five Poems. Includes the translation from Yiddish of Rosenfeld's "The Teardrop Millionaire." Set to music by Irwin Heilner. Sung by Mary Sarnoff, soprano. 21 Oct. 1975.

Two Songs. Translations from German of Goethe's "First Loss" and Heine's "It's Getting Dark." Set to music by Michael Cherry. Sung by Vincent Arnone, tenor. Manhattan School of Music, NY. 11 May 1976.

O Golden Land! Kramer reads selections from his recently published 1963 travelog in verse and provides introductory material. Also includes excerpts from his translation from German of Heinrich Heine's "Germany: A Winter's Tale," which he acknowledges as the model for his own poem. A Spoken Words Program. WNYC, New York. 21 Dec. 1976.

Songs of the Ghettos. "Never Say." Arranged by Arieh Levanon, based on a Russian folk song. Performed by the Renanim Singers. Hirsh Glik's "Partisan Song" translated from Yiddish by Kramer, who is identified as "Aron Cramer" on the album jacket. Hed Arzi, Israel, PRT-14586, 1976. Phonograph record.

Ten Songs. Includes translations from German of Heine's "A New Song" set to music by Doris Bauman and Brecht's "Wiegenlied" set to music by Hanns Eisler as well as a translation from Yiddish of Rosenfeld's "My Little Son" set to music by Irwin Heilner. Sung by Viki Ann Diamond, soprano. 2 May 1977.

The Emperor of Atlantis: Interviews and Songs. Host Robert Sherman interviews director Ian Strasfogel, conductor Kerry Woodward, and translator Aaron Kramer who comment on the artistic merit as well as the historical significance of the opera by Viktor Ullmann and Peter Kien. Sherman also presents seven excerpts from the opera performed live by members of the New Opera Theatre cast. A Listening Room Program. WQXR, New York, 11 May 1977.

The Emperor of Atlantis. An opera composed by Viktor Ullmann and written by Peter Kien at the concentration camp in Terezin, Czechoslovakia in 1944. Translated from German by Kramer. Performed by the New Opera Theatre. Directed by Ian Strasfogel. Conducted by Kerry Woodward. World premiere one month earlier by the San Francisco Opera, San Francisco, CA. Brooklyn Academy Of Music, Brooklyn. 22 May 1977.

Aaron Kramer Reads the 'Emperor of Atlantis'. Kramer reads his translation from German of Peter Kien's libretto. He also provides an introduction to the work and discusses its creation in the concentration camp at Terezin. A Spoken Words Program. WNYC, New York. 10 Nov. 1977.

Jewish Voices. Kramer provides an introduction and reads his translations from Yiddish of Winchevsky, Edelshtat and others. He then reads from forty years of his own verse on Jewish themes. Introduced by Stanley Barkan as part of a series presented by Cross-Cultural Communications. Merrick Public Library, Merrick, NY. 12 May 1978.

Death Takes a Holiday. Kramer's script describes cultural life in the concentration camp of Terezin and explains how the opera, Der Kaiser Von Atlantis, was created there in 1944. Commissioned to coincide with the broadcast premiere of the British Broadcasting Corporation's production of Kramer's translation from German of The Emperor of Atlantis. Produced by Piers Plowright. British Broadcasting Company. 27 Feb. 1979.

Rilke: Visions of Christ, Part One. Kramer introduces and reads his translations from German of Visions of Christ. He quotes at length from Siegfried Mandel's introduction to the volume. WBAI, New York. 19 Mar. 1979.

Rilke: Visions of Christ, Part Two. Kramer reads the remaining poems of the cycle. WBAI, New York. 26 Mar. 1979.

The Variety and Strength of Yiddish Poetry. Kramer illustrates his YKUF lecture with many of his translations from Yiddish, including a series of newly translated lullabies from an Israeli anthology. Recording includes only the first half of the lecture. Los Angeles. 19 May 1979.

Forms of Resistance: Anti-McCarthy poems of Aaron Kramer. Kramer includes several translations from Yiddish to illustrate his response to the events of that era. WBAI, New York. 1 Oct. 1979.

Yiddish Lullabies. Kramer reads and discusses his translations from the Israeli anthology Unter Yankele's Vigele. A Spoken Words Program. WNYC, New York. 28 June 1981.

"My Poems Are Full of Poison" Set to music by Irwin Heilner and arranged by Walter Spalding. Performed by Bonnie Feather, soprano; Charles Spining, piano; and Walter Spalding, classical guitar. Heine's poem translated from German. Capriccio Concert. Flagstaff, AZ. 31 Dec. 1981.

(Songs) Translations from Yiddish and German set to music by Heilner, Schrogin, and Heller. Sung by Bets Vondrasek, soprano. South Huntington Public Library, South Huntington, NY. 6 May 1984.

Poetry of the Holocaust. Robert Ballantine and Kramer discuss the Nazi holocaust and other holocausts. Kramer reads his own and other translations of holocaust poetry. WBAU, Garden City, NY. 24 Oct. 1984.

Poetry of the Holocaust. Kramer reads many of his translations which were later to appear in A Century of Yiddish Poetry. Bets Vondrasek sings four of his translations. Bayshore/Brightwater's Public Library, Bayshore, NY. 19 May 1985.

Heine: Balladeer of the People. Several of Kramer's Heine translations are sung. Kramer reads and discusses some of Heine's narrative poems. Unitarian Universalist Fellowship, Garden City, NY. 15 Sep. 1985.

Four Songs from the Yiddish. Translated by Kramer. Set to music by Waldemar Hille. Sung by Kathy Roche-Zujko. First Unitarian Church, Los Angeles. 3 Aug. 1986.

Babi Yar. Set to music by Muriel Roth. Premiered in Santa Fe, NM. Mar. 1986.

The Poet and the Art of Translation: Siv Cedering and Aaron Kramer. Kramer reads and discusses his translations from German, Yiddish, and Hungarian. Poetry Center, C.W. Post College, Greenvale, NY. 11 Mar. 1987.

(Poetry Reading) Kramer reads and discusses many Yiddish, German, and Hungarian translations. Donnell Library, NY. 5 May 1987.

Three Yiddish Lullabies. Translated by Kramer. Set to music by Judith Berman. Sung by cantor Samuel Brown. 13 Apr. 1988.

Aaron Kramer. Interview. Jewish Community Hour. With Estelle D. Abraham. Kramer reads and discusses several of his translations from Yiddish. WNTR, Washington, DC. 30 July 1988.

Yiddish Poets of Social Conscience. A lecture reading by Kramer of many poems from A Century of Yiddish Poetry. County Line Unitarian Universalist Fellowship, Amityville, NY. 18 Sep. 1988.

An Evening with Dr. Aaron Kramer. Kramer reads and discusses nineteen translations from A Century of Yiddish Poetry. Introduction by library director Sara Courant. Patchogue-Medford Public Library, Patchogue, NY. 17 Oct. 1988. Videotape.

Yiddish Poets of Labor. Kramer reads selections from the first section of A Century of Yiddish Poetry. WBAI, New York. 1 May 1990.

CHECKLIST OF ARTICLES ABOUT KRAMER TRANSLATIONS:

Redman, Ben Ray. "Master of the living word." **SATURDAY REVIEW** 4 Dec. 1948: 40-1.

Rolfs, Alvin R. "Heine, Poet of Wit, Love and Freedom." **ST. LOUIS POST-DISPATCH** 12 Dec. 1948: n. pag.

Werner, Alfred. "A Portable Heine." **CONGRESS WEEKLY** 20 Dec. 1948: n. pag.

Bradley, Lyman R. "Heine as Realist." **MASSES AND MAINSTREAM** Jan. 1949: n. pag.

Daiches, David. "Symbol and poet." **NEW REPUBLIC** 14 Feb. 1949: 24-5.

Fast, Howard. "Poet of the Jewish workers." **JEWISH LIFE** July 1955: 20.

Green, Ber. "Morris Rosenfeld's Poems in English." Rev. of The Teardrop Millionaire. **MORNING FREIHEIT** 30 Oct. 1955: 10. In Yiddish.

Benedict, Michael. "The shapes of nature." **POETRY** Dec. 1968: 209.

Kirsch, Robert. "Rilke's Christ narratives published for the first time." **LOS ANGELES TIMES** 28 Aug. 1968: Section IV, 2.

Lenel, Edith. Rev. of Visions of Christ. **LIBRARY JOURNAL** 1 Nov. 1968: 4145.

Commanday, Robert. "A bold striking Emperor at Spring Opera." **SAN FRANCISCO CHRONICLE** 23 Apr. 1977: 34.

Saal, Hubert. "Death takes a holiday." **NEWSWEEK** 16 May 1977: 116-7.

Rockwell, John. "New opera theater offering work of Argento and Ullmann." **NEW YORK TIMES** 21 May 1977: 11.

Porter, Andrew. "A lecture and a parable." **NEW YORKER** 6 June 1977: 111-2.

Wickstrom, Gordon. "The Emperor of Atlantis: satire in the Nazi concentration camps." **THEATRE JOURNAL** Oct. 1980: 386-7.

Delatiner, Barbara. "A Yiddishist with a passion." **NEW YORK TIMES** 9 Oct. 1988, Long Island sec.: 24-5.

Lerner, Arthur. "Putting Yiddish poetry in focus." **HERITAGE: SOUTHWEST JEWISH PRESS** (Los Angeles) 10 Mar. 1989, Viewpoint: D.

Black, Harold. "Translator salvaged Yiddish poetry in monumental work." Rev. of A Century of Yiddish Poetry. Washington (DC) **JEWISH WEEK** 20 April 1989: 25. Condensed version in Visions #30 June 1989.

Kaufman, Marjorie. "A Century of Yiddish Poetry: Yiddish poetry - silenced for years." **THREE VILLAGE HERALD** (East Setauket, NY) 24 May 1989: 19+

Rosenfeld, Rita. Rev. of A Century of Yiddish Poetry. **OUTLOOK** July-Aug. 1989: 16-17.

Baxter, Robert. "'Emperor' bears compelling stamp of Nazi camp." **COURIER-POST** (Philadelphia, PA) 20 Nov. 1989: n. pag.

Webster, Daniel. "At Curtis, a paradoxical opera of life and death." **THE PHILADELPHIA INQUIRER** 23 Nov. 1989: n. pag.

Valencia, Heather. "A Cornucopia of Yiddish poetry." **JEWISH QUARTERLY** (London) Spring 1990: 57-61.

Rosenfeld, Max. "Our Yiddish poetic heritage." **JEWISH CURRENTS** Jun. 1990: 26-8.

Notes on Contributors

SAM ABRAMS is a professor of language and literature at the Rochester Institute of Technology. He was jailed during the Vietnam War for his role as a protestor. Scholar in residence at Richmond College in London during 1993, his latest book is **THE NEGLECTED WALT WHITMAN**.

ABRAHAM ALMANY, born in Haifa, Israel, was a member of the Irgun Zvai Leumi from 1938 to 1948, and was imprisoned in Kenya and Eritrea from December 1944 to July 1948 for activities in that organization. He emigrated to the United States in 1958, and is currently Professor Emeritus of Political Science at Dowling College.

W. H. AUDEN, born in England, came to the United States in 1939. He received the 1948 Pulitzer Prize in poetry. Returning to England as professor of poetry at Oxford University in 1956, he became poet in residence there in 1972. He died in 1973 in Vienna, Austria.

MIRIAM BAKER, a professor of English at Dowling College, is an expert on the teaching of writing. She is a graduate of Smith College, and taught at the State University of New York at Stony Brook before joining the faculty at Dowling College.

STANLEY BARKAN is editor-in-chief of Cross-Cultural Communications, publishers of bilingual literature focusing on cultures in contact. The publishing house is located in Merrick, New York.

DICK BARNES, poet and musician, teaches at Pomona College. His next major project in translation, undertaken with his former colleague Carl W. Ernst, will be a survey of medieval poetry from Judaism, Christianity and Islam.

WALTER M. BARZELAY, an Israeli poet, one of that country's most widely translated writers, having been published in Arabic, Italian, Japanese, Portuguese, Russian and Swedish, among other languages. He died in 1987 near Moscow.

HAROLD BLACK was an urban planner until retiring to become a full-time writer. He has published two books of poetry, **HERITAGE** and **MY FATHER ABRAHAM**, and several translations of poems from Spanish and Yiddish.

FREDERICK BRAININ was born in Vienna in 1913, and emigrated to the United States in 1938. He served in the United States Army during World War II. He is anthologized in American, Austrian and Israeli collections of poetry. His home is New York City.

JOHN BRANDER lived for many years in South Africa. An attorney, he has published extensively on life in that region, including **THE TRAIL OF THE MOON** and **CHILDREN PLAYING BY THE SIDE OF HELL**, both collections of poetry. He now lives in Scotland.

RICHARD EMIL BRAUN grew up four blocks from the corner where Detroit began burning. Author of two books of poetry and two verse novels, he is the translator of Sophocles' **ANTIGONE**, Euripides' **RHESOS**, and Persius' **SATIRES**.

JEROME BROOKS is a professor of English at the City College of the City University of New York. From 1976 until 1978, he was a senior

Fulbright lecturer in American civilization at the University of Madagascar.

JONATHAN COHEN has published translations of several Latin American poets, including Cardenal, Lihn and Paz. He was awarded a 1989 grant from the New York State Council on the arts for the completion of his translation of Pedro Mir's "Countersong".

CARLOS CUNHA teaches political science at Dowling College, and has taught in Haiti. He has published several articles and a book on the Portuguese Communist Party.

RHONDA CUNHA is a studio artist on Long Island specializing in sculpture and drawing. She has exhibited nationally and internationally. She has lived in Haiti, and her work reflects her interests in that region.

EVA FEILER was an associate editor with Cross-Cultural Communications at the time of her death in 1986. Born in Romania in 1933, she managed to emigrate to Israel before coming to the United States, where she earned her doctorate in Comparative Literature at New York University. Her translation of Nina Cassian's **BLUE APPLE** was the first English translation of poetry by the renowned Romanian poet.

EDWARD FIELD has translated Inuit literature for many years, and one of his translations appeared in New York subways and buses as part of the Poetry in Motion series. His latest book is **COUNTING MYSELF LUCKY, SELECTED POEMS 1963 - 1992** (Black Sparrow Press, 1992).

CHARLES FISHMAN is a Distinguished Service Professor of English and Humanities at the State University of New York in Farmingdale, where he has directed the Visiting Writers Program since 1979. He has published several books of poetry, including **BLOOD TO REMEMBER: AMERICAN POETS ON THE HOLOCAUST**.

PAUL FORCHHEIMER, an ordained rabbi, lives in New York. He was born in Germany, and has taught German and Linguistics.

ROBERT FRIEND has published six books of poetry, the latest **DANCING WITH A TIGER** (1990), and three books of poetry translated from the Hebrew of Leah Goldberg, Natan Alterman, and Gabriel Preil. Born in New York, he has been in Israel since 1950, and taught English Literature at the Hebrew University for more than thirty years.

DONALD GILZINGER, Aaron Kramer's bibliographer, teaches English at Suffolk Community College on Long Island.

DANIELA GIOSEFFI has been publishing poetry and prose for the past two decades. She is the author of **THE GREAT AMERICAN BELLY** (New York and London: Doubleday), and the anthology she edited, **WOMEN ON WAR: INTERNATIONAL VOICES** (New York: Simon and Schuster) received an American Book Award in 1990.

FRITZ HENSEY teaches linguistics and translation studies in the Department of Spanish and Portuguese at the University of Texas at Austin. A professional translator, he has published several books and articles on issues in linguistics, and is a published poet.

EDWIN HONIG, professor of English at Brown University, is an experienced translator of Portuguese and Spanish poetry.

PAUL T. HOPPER taught German and humanities for several years. He has been a translator of non-fiction prose from German, Russian and Italian since 1980.

DAVID IGNATOW was born in 1914, and published his first volume of poetry in 1948. He has since published fourteen more volumes of poetry, and several volumes of prose, the most recent in 1994. He was awarded the Bollingen Prize in 1977.

SHIRLEY KAUFMAN has lived in Jerusalum since 1973. She has published several volumes of translations of contemporary Israeli poets and five collections of her own poetry, most recently **RIVERS OF SALT** (Copper Canyon Press, 1993).

STEPHEN KLASS, professor of English at Adelphi University, has translated the epic poem **ADAM HOMO** by F. Paludan-Muller, and collaborated with Leif Sjoberg on a translation of Harry Martinson's **ANIARA**. He is currently translating novels by Sara Lidman.

AARON KRAMER, in whose honor this book was compiled, first gained national attention with **SEVEN POETS IN SEARCH OF AN ANSWER**, published in 1944. Donald Gilzinger's bibliographical essay in this volume does not extend to 1991, the year in which Aaron published **INDIGO**, a collection of poetry.

NORBERT KRAPF is professor of English at the C.W. Post Campus of Long Island University. He is the author of several collections of poetry, and has had his translations of German drama produced in Ohio and Indiana.

CARRIE LECAKES is a former student of Aaron Kramer's. She is studying Modern Greek poetry, and now resides in Colorado.

SEYMOUR LEVITAN's translations of Yiddish poems and stories are included in numerous anthologies. **PAPER ROSES**, his selection and translation of Rachel Korn's poetry, was the 1988 winner of the Robert Payne Award of the Translation Center at Columbia University. He lives in Vancouver, British Columbia.

SIEGFRIED MANDEL is Professor Emeritus of English and Comparative Literature at the University of Colorado in Boulder. He is the author of **RANIER MARIA RILKE** among others, and with Aaron Kramer, the first to translate a large body of Ingeborg Bachman's poems.

CHARLES MIZZI is currently lecturing at the University of Malta, where he was born. He is married to Dr. Sibyl Mizzi, an anthropologist. A paratrooper in World War II, he enjoyed forty years teaching in American schools and colleges.

RAYMOND PATTERSON is the author of several collections of poetry, and is a professor of English at the City College of the City University of New York.

PAMELA PERRY is a specialist in Bulgarian folksong and dance, and is fluent in Bulgarian, Serbo-Croatian and Russian. She is married to a Bulgarian musicologist, and lives in Washington, D.C.

CHARLES PLUMB lived for many years in Mallorca, Spain. Known as a translator of Classical, Spanish and Mallorquin literature, he was widely acclaimed for his translations of Lorca's poetry. He died in Mallorca in 1992.

PREM PRASAD, born in India, received doctorate and master's degrees from Columbia University. She holds an Honors Degree in Hindi from Panjab University, and translated stories by Maupassant and Chekhov into that language for radio production. She lives on Long Island.

ANTONIA RAPTIS is a former student of Aaron Kramer's. She is an elementary school teacher.

P. N. REMLER is an American diplomat with experience in many parts of the Turkic world.

LUIS EDUARDO RIVERA is a professor of finance at Dowling College. He specializes in banking policy in Spain. He is the son of the poet he translated for in this book.

MARINA ROSCHER, born in Germany, is a professional translator, and a founding member of the **NEW YORK QUARTERLY**. She is a widely published essayist, poet and fiction writer.

SUSAN L. ROSENSTREICH teaches foreign languages at Dowling College. Her poetry and translations have been published in anthologies.

RUTH RUBIN is a folklorist with broad experience in Yiddish folksongs and culture. As a field collector, she gathered material now in The Library of Congress, The YIVO Institute of Jewish Research, and Museum Hatefutsoth in Israel. She is the author of **VOICES OF THE PEOPLE: THE STORY OF YIDDISH FOLKSONG.**

VERN RUTSALA teaches at Lewis and Clark College, and has published eight collections of poetry, the most recent of which, **SELECTED POEMS**, received the Hazel Hall Award. He has been a Guggenheim Fellow, and was twice awarded NEA grants.

SHIMON SANDBANK was born in Tel-Aviv, studied English literature in Jerusalem and Cambridge, and is professor of English and comparative literature at the Hebrew University of Jerusalem. He has published Hebrew translations of **THE CANTERBURY TALES** and Shakespeare's **SONNETS.**

JAMES SCHEVILL, poet and playwright, published two books in 1993: **FIVE PLAYS** (The Swallow Press, Ohio University Press) and **BERN PORTER: A PERSONAL BIOGRAPHY** (Gardiner, Maine: Tilbury House Publishers).

LEIF SJOBERG collaborated with W.H. Auden, Muriel Rukeyser, May Swenson, William Jay Smith and Stephen Klass on translating several books of poetry from Swedish. He has written on Gunnar Ekelof and Par Lagerkvist, and is Professor Emeritus of Scandinavian Studies and Comparative Literature at the State University of New York at Stony Brook.

WILLIAM STAFFORD became a recognized poet in the 1950's, and his many collections were published principally by Harper Collins. He made his home in Lake Oswego, Oregon until his death in 1993. He and Yorifumi Yaguchi had been friends and collaborators for years.

ANN STEINMETZ is professor of speech and communication arts at Dowling College. Her special interest is ethnography.

BRADLEY STRAHAN teaches poetry at Georgetown University, and is director of Visions International Arts. His work includes several books of poetry and over 400 of his poems have been published in periodicals and anthologies around the world. He is widely translated.

TIMEA SZELL was born in Hungary, and emigrated to the United States at the age of seventeen. She teaches English at Barnard College, specializing in medieval English literature, creative writing and women's studies. Her fiction has appeared in several journals.

JOHN TAGLIABUE, born in Italy, became interested in China during his student days at Columbia University, when he purchased a copy of Lin Yuang's Wisdom of China and India. He is Professor Emeritus of English at Bates College, and has taught in Japan, China and Greece, among other places.

MARTIN TUCKER editor of **CONFRONTATION**, a literary journal, is Professor of English at C. W. Post College of Long Island University. He is the author of **HOMES OF LOCKS AND MYSTERIES**, a book of poetry, **LITERARY EXILE IN THE TWENTIETH CENTURY, AFRICA IN MODERN LITERATURE, SAM SHEPARD**, and **JOSEPH CONRAD**.

BARRY WALLENSTEIN is the author of four collections of poetry, the most recent of which is **THE SHORT LIFE OF THE FIVE MINUTE DANCER** (Ridgeway Press, 1993). He teaches literature and creative writing at the City College in New York.

CLAIRE NICOLAS WHITE, novelist, poet, and translator, was born in the Netherlands. She is the author of **THE DEATH OF THE ORANGE TREES**, a novel published by Harper and Rowe, **BIOGRAPHY AND OTHER POEMS**, and **FRAGMENTS OF STAINED GLASS**.

YORIFUMI YAGUCHI is a poet and university professor. The author of nine collections of poetry, he has also translated poems of Rin Ishigaki, Sachiko Yoshihara and Shuntaro Tanikawa into English with William Stafford. He is an editor of **POETRY NIPPON**, and lives in Sapporo.

SACHIKO YOSHIHARA was born in Tokyo in 1932. She studied French Literature at Tokyo University. She is one of Japan's most active poets, and has published several collections of poetry. Of these, **CHILDHOOD LITANY** received the Muroo Saisei Prize in 1965, and **BINDWEED** received the Takami Jun Prize in 1974.

ELIO ZAPPULLA is a professor of English at Dowling College. He is a translator of Italian poetry, and his translation of Dante's **INFERNO** is to be published soon by Random House.

LINDA ZISQUIT is a poet and a translator of Israeli poetry. Her most recent book is **RITUAL BATH**, a collection of her poetry published by Broken Moon Press in 1992.